POLISH INVASION

by

KSAWERY PRUSZYŃSKI

BIRLINN

This edition published in 2009 by
Birlinn Limited
West Newington House
10 Newington Road
Edinburgh
EH9 1QS

www.birlinn.co.uk

First published in 1941 by
Minerva Publishing Company, London

Translation by Peter Jordan
Introduction © copyright Neal Ascherson 2009

The Publisher would like to acknowledge the assistance of the
Pruszyński family in preparing the new edition of this book

ISBN: 978 1 84341 048 5

Facsimile origination by Brinnoven, Livingston
Printed and bound by Cox & Wyman Ltd, Reading

Ksaw

own home in what is now Byelorussia. After serving
the forces in Scotland, he became a diplomat and—although
never a Communist—returned to Poland after the war to
serve the new Soviet-dominated government at the United
Nations and then as ambassador to the Netherlands. But
Sovict intelligence never trusted him, and in 1950 he was
killed in a car crash in Germany which may not have been
an accident.

Neal Ascherson was born in Edinburgh and studied at Cam-
bridge University. A journalist for many years, he has also
published numerous books and is well known as an authority on Polish and East European affairs.

CONTENTS

INTRODUCTION

The Scots were until recently accustomed to think of themselves as an emigrant nation. With the great exception of the Irish immigration into the industrial west of Scotland in the 19th century, they had almost no experience of hosting a large group of non-Scots until the Second World War. So the arrival in 1940 of tens of thousands of Polish servicemen—soldiers, sailors and airmen—was an enormous and ultimately liberating cultural shock. Vividly "foreign", with their exotic uniforms and strange language, the Poles spread out across camps and bases mainly in the east and south-east of Scotland.

In the course of their stay, which was to last almost five years, they injected Scottish rural and small-town life with a new excitement which is still remembered—mostly very fondly—by the older generation. As one woman wrote to *The Herald* the other day, commenting on the latest influx of young Poles: "Nobody has mentioned one important reason for welcoming Poles, but perhaps only ladies in their late seventies know it. They can all dance like Fred Astaire."

They were the survivors of the Polish forces who had fought the Germans in their own country and then fought them again in France in 1940. Churchill decreed that the troops who escaped across the Channel after the fall of France should be based in Scotland. Here they guarded the coast against invasion, retrained and eventually took part in the Allied landings in Normandy and the campaigns which

followed. Many of the men came from Poland's eastern prov-
inces which had been seized by the Soviet Union in 1939,
and after the war, thousands chose to remain in Scotland.

With them came the well-known writer Ksawery
Pruszyński, a radical journalist who had lost his own home
in what is now Byelorussia. After serving with the forces
in Scotland, he became a diplomat and—although never
a Communist—returned to Poland after the war to serve
the new Communist-dominated government at the United
Nations and then as ambassador to the Netherlands. But
Soviet intelligence never trusted him, and in 1950 he was
killed in a car crash in Germany which may not have been
an accident.

This little book, first published in 1941, is a witty and
perceptive account of the mutual impact of Poles and Scots
in wartime Scotland. As he says, real affection grew out of
initial misunderstanding: "[the Pole] took the other for a
kind of Englishman, and was rewarded by being taken for a
kind of Russian." He records warm Scottish hospitality and
friendships in which each side tried to explain the complex-
ities of their national history to the other. And he chronicles
passionate debates among the Poles as their Catholic padres
and local Church of Scotland ministers struggled vainly to
control the outrageous success of Polish charm with Scottish
girls. The soldiers paid little attention.

"What will be left for the women of Poland?"

"We will manage to have something left for them."

The book ends with a happy vision which now, in
hindsight, reads with piteous irony. The Poles plan a huge
ceremony of gratitude after the war, in which all the Scots
who have shown them such kindness will arrive in ships
escorted by the Polish navy, to be welcomed throughout the
free nation. But the reality, which even Pruszyński could not

foresee, was to be a brutal dictatorship in which all soldiers who had fought in the West, and their Scottish wives, were treated as enemies of the people and potential traitors.

Today, young Poles and Scots are better acquainted than they have ever been. And the long history of Scottish association with Poland, going back many centuries, is at last being retrieved by historians. Thanks to the initiative of Birlinn, the publishers, Ksawery Pruszyński's touching and unforgettable contribution to that mutual history can be read once more.

Neal Ascherson
August 2009

Chapter 1

DISASTER

MARSHAL PETAIN'S Government applied two days
ago to the *Reichskanzler* for an armistice. The Chancellor accepted the offer, but the armoured divisions did not
break their march across France—only the French defence
collapsed everywhere. The German tidal wave reached
Orleans and Tours, Rennes and Dijon, the valleys of the
Rhone and of the Loire. The straight roads of France
were filled with fugitives from the north. Weeping women
and lost children mingled with army deserters. Disarmed,
but still in uniform, French soldiers tried to forget their
shame in cafés and drown it in wine. Some of them
cheered the welcome slogan : " *La guerre est finie !* "

But there was in one corner of France a different scene.
In the small harbours of the Atlantic coast, of South Brittany,
of Vandée and of sandy Gascogne, there were different
men and other sights. The tiny ports facing the great
ocean and backed by ancient little towns had long forgotten
the meaning of the word " war." They had never seen it
since Cardinal Richelieu's expedition against the last
hardy citadel of Protestants, La Rochelle. And then they
remembered also the dark days of the fourth year of
Revolution, when relief from overseas for the Chouans of
Vandée was landed on their narrow quays and when they
were the last strongholds of resistance against the Con-
vention of Paris.

And now they were full of troops. Their quaint squares
and streets were swarming with soldiers. There were
soldiers everywhere, but they were all going towards the
quays and jetties. They were fully armed. They waved

aside the gendarmes' request to lay down arms and they thought little of the desperate entreaties of the mayor, who had just followed the example of Paris itself in declaring his borough an open town. They just did not listen to French persuasion—and they were strong enough not to fear anything other than persuasion. If they answered at all, they did so in terms which no Frenchman could fail to understand and appreciate—the words of General Cambronne of the Emperor's Old Guard.

They were left alone.

" *Que voulez-vous, ce sont des Polonais ; ils n'ont jamais ete raisonnables,*" said the mayor.

" *C'est à eux que nous devons tout ça,*" added with sudden venom a plump gentleman with a share-pusher's manner, who was very busy getting some petrol for his Hispano.

As though Danzig was ever more than a shadow of an excuse for Hitler's war !

But an old woman of Brittany, with a face wrinkled like a shrivelled orange, daughter, wife and mother of sailors, looked at the armed men with other eyes : " *Que la sainte Vierge vous garde, les gars, hé !* "

Les gars looked at her. They happened to be not those of France, but those who had arrived a few months earlier, after a long trek from Poland over the mountains, through Rumania, Bulgaria, the Mediterranean and Greece —young lads. They did not understand much French; but the old woman's smile told them all.

She blessed them with a broad sign of the cross. Just as the Bishop of Oléron has been blessing for many hundred years the fishing craft of Quimper sailing on the high seas.

* *
*

In the consulates of unheard-of South American republics ; in Bordeaux, crammed with fine cars and people ; in Saint Jean de Luz, scorched by the summer sun, the crowd of international refugees was swelling and throbbing. Pale, frightened faces, stripped bare of yesterday's arrogance and contorted with anxiety. Struggling for visas. Most fantastic, most exotic visas. Traders in passports. Brokers in permits. Expert discussions about current prices and values.

" Venezuela ? "

" The Portuguese don't give transits for Venezuela."

" Oh. . . ."

" I've got a Curaçao."

" Where is this Curaçao ? "

" ? . . . ."

" You can't get Chinese ones any more. . . ."

" Not here, but you might get one in Marseilles."

" Are there trains to Marseilles ? "

" Yes, but the Italians are there. . . ."

" . . . ."

Refugees from Vienna and Prague, from Amsterdam and Paris, speaking bad French and indifferent German, a cosmopolitan, miserable, scared babel of fear, dreaming of unattainable Manhattan and staring far into the sea or towards the Pyrenean frontier as to a Promised Land.

Someone whispered : " The British ships are here ! British ships are coming ! "

A husky, sceptical voice asked, " What British ships ? "

" They came to fetch the Polish soldiers. They will take them to England. Perhaps we might go there, too ? Just for a beginning."

The heavy voice laughed ironically : " To England ? Let the British go there if they like. You would have to be mad like the Poles to want to go to England now."

And the crowd, after a short shiver of excited hope, settled down again in the long queue leading to the desk of the fishy-looking clerk of an equally disreputable-looking consulate.

* *

Lifeboats, fishing smacks, pontoons—every kind of craft was used by the soldiers, climbing hastily on board, anxious to leave land. There were among them some

Frenchmen and a good many Czechs. Republican
Spaniards who had escaped from an internment camp
came to the Polish officers and begged : " The British
sailors have orders to take only Poles. Nothing was said
about Spaniards. Take us with you as Poles. Let us
join your force."

There was some hesitation.

" You will not be ashamed of us, sir. We were at
Guadalajara."

Some greatcoats and caps did double duty. Mixed with
Poles, some Spaniards jumped into the British launch.
The forage caps with Polish eagles looked odd on the
heads of olive-skinned Castillians, but there was no time
for racial study.

Quickly the launch unloaded its human cargo and
returned to the shore, where others were impatiently
waiting.

There were all kinds of ships, most of them British, some
from the old Polish mercantile marine, some Dutch,
some taken from the Germans. There were big liners and
dirty tramps. Some were fast and some quite slow. It was
a fleet resembling that of Dunkerque of some weeks
before.

" *Ne pars pas ! Reste !* "—a young, dark French girl
was crying and clutching her Polish soldier.

" Don't go ! Stay here ! You will get rid of the
uniform and live with us. My people liked you. Father
hauls in a thousand francs worth of fish a day in the season
and you will help him. We've got four boats, you know.
Stay here. Why go to England, why go to war ? They
will sink your ship, the Boches. Everyone says so. They
are sure to sink you. Why, if they could take Paris. . . ."

Her words were drowned in the babel. He gave her
a strong, brief kiss of farewell and jumped into the launch.
But his heart was heavy and his mouth bitter. He waved
a rough, hard workman's hand to the girl who was biting
a red silk scarf, standing alone and helpless on the quay.

The boat swayed in the swell, for there were no jetties and breakwaters in the small harbour. Many Poles lost confidence when they left the firm foothold of the land. They could not help it. Theirs was not a seafaring nation and some of them saw the ocean for the first time in their lives when they arrived from Coetquidan.

After the launch bobbing over the waves, the British cruiser seemed as solid and steady as land itself. They climbed on board. The soldier who had just said goodbye to his girl slipped on the gangway and nearly fell into the water, but he was held up at the last moment by a strong hand. As soon as he stood on his own feet, he turned to see his friend. He was a tall bluejacket, red haired and broad shouldered, grinning with white teeth : " Polish, good ! Good ! " And then, showing off : " Polish—dobra ! " And he produced some cigarettes.

The Pole, not to be outdone, searched for some English words and said : " Englishman, good, good ! "

He was amazed to see the British sailor wagging his head in earnest, good-natured denial : " No. No Englishman," he tried to explain, " No Englishman ; Scottish, Scotsman, Scotland." There was great surprise. The Pole, a village boy from Sandomierz, could not understand it at all. People knew little about the world in his village. He had been working for the last two years on a farm near Toulouse, but the French did not help him very much to extend his geographical knowledge. " Well, things must have gone topsy-turvy in this world if this English sailor is not an Englishman ! " he thought.

Others were as amazed as he was and someone tried to explain the strange phenomenon : " You know, in the North of England, of that island, there is a nation called the Scots. They speak English, but they are different. They wear their own costume and all the men go about in skirts. Haven't you seen pictures in the newspapers ? The English say the Scots can look after their pennies better than anyone. And one Polish aspirant who speaks

English says that we are sailing to Scotland to rebuild our army there. So we shall find out about those Scots."

Such was the encounter between the sons of a Slav nation and the Celts of the North. A meeting between the people from the Vistula plains, the mountains of Podhale, the forests of Pomorze and the rich fields of Poznan with the people of the Highlands, of the Clyde and the Tay.

Each knew very little about the other, and what they knew was often untrue. The one took the other for a kind of Englishman and was rewarded by being taken for a kind of Russian. But war is a great teacher of geography, helping to make discoveries hardly less startling than those of Columbus or of Cook.

The engines were already throbbing ahead. The coast of France, a land over which the German tide was crawling farther every minute, grew faint in the mist and from the unknown a new land of Polish war pilgrimage began to emerge—Scotland.

Chapter 2

BACK UNDER CANVAS

EVERYTHING came back to normal. They lived again in various temporary camps in suburban parks, on former exhibition grounds, racecourses, in the courtyards of abandoned factories or in big farms. It was a cold and wet summer, recalling the autumn of the previous year. Vivid memories came into their minds. Balaton, Lengyel-furdo, Mohacs, in Hungary ; Tulcza, Babadag, Targo-viste, in Rumania ; Palangas, in Lithuania, and many others in Estonia, Latvia, Jugoslavia.

Of course, there was a difference. They were now in an Allied country which was still fighting. The other countries were sympathetic at most, but they tried to use the screen of neutrality as a shield against the misfortune which had overcome a neighbour. They were anxious lest any display of friendly feeling towards the remnants of a once glorious army should bring on them the wrath of Germany.

Now things were different. But the memory of the second war cataclysm they had seen within a year was fresh. The knowledge that the lesson of Poland had been wasted was bitter. For the second time they had had to escape from the midst of the enemy armoured columns and to see the break-up of regiments, divisions, armies. And now this waiting of the amorphous human mass which had been an army and might still become one, this waiting for an unknown fate, reminded them of the months spent in the autumn of 1939 in Rumanian, Hungarian or Lithuanian camps.

They could not help being depressed. For the British the collapse of France meant the first direct menace to their home territory. For the French it meant as much as September 1939 had for the Poles. But for the Poles it was the re-enactment of the tragedy ; it meant the tearing open of fresh wounds. The only Continental Power opposing Germany ceased to exist. New nails were driven into the lid of Poland's coffin.

And there was still another reason for gloom. In Rumania and Hungary, even in France, one used to get, from time to time, news from home, sometimes horrible, sometimes comforting. But now the last link had snapped and the secret, underground channels by which news leaked through to France were hopelessly barred. There was no hope of any news, bad or good. No one knew how long this state would last.

" Ah, if only the German offensive had started two weeks earlier or two weeks later," said someone.

" What difference could it make ? "

" A very big difference to us," the other man replied. " If it had started a fortnight earlier our two divisions trained in Brittany during the winter would not have gone to the front line and they could have been shipped to England intact. They would have been much stronger now."

" And what if the German offensive had started later ? "

" If it had started later we would probably have had time to mobilise more Poles in France. You know that the French coal industry objected to the calling up of a larger number of the Polish miners from the North of France. Later on we might have got those men. Everything was ready for their reception. We had the officers to train them. But before they came the Germans broke through, just in the North, where the Poles were."

He was perfectly right. That is why there were so many officers among the refugees from France.

The Polish camp of Coetquidan in Brittany was a great military factory producing soldiers. It had sent two divisions and one motorised brigade to the Western Front, as well as another brigade to Narvik in Norway. Two new divisions were in course of formation and others were being prepared. That is why there were many officers, waiting for the organisation of new units.

* *

The first Polish camps in Great Britain were close to ports and every now and then there were new arrivals from the sea. A part of the Highland Brigade which had been at Narvik landed in a British port. Various cutters and fishing boats brought from France Polish soldiers, who often set out at night with scarcely any knowledge of sailing or navigation and yet eventually reached England. Perhaps some of those who started never did arrive, but who knows how many tried ? Some others sailed a yacht from the Mediterranean through the Straits of Gibraltar. Others found their way to Casablanca or Dakar and came to Britain from there. Many went through Spain and Portugal. They met adventure on a thousand incredible routes from France to Britain.

Some Polish soldiers escaped from prison camps, sometimes during their transfer to Germany. Some managed to travel across the whole of Germany, from Poland to Brussels, riding on the axles of railway trucks, and then were overtaken in Belgium by the rush of armoured divisions. Surf-riding on the crest of the terrific wave, hiding among motor transport columns and passing for Germans, they reached unoccupied France and thence England.

Some, knowing no Spanish at all, tramped across the whole of Spain, from Irun to Vigo, choosing mountain roads.

The most fantastic visas were obtained in order to get the transit permits from neutrals. The ostensible destination of the travellers was the Dutch or Belgian colonies, China or Central America. The consular officials were at first surprised by the sudden enthusiasm of the Poles for exotic countries. But nothing can remain long hidden from diplomats.

"Yes," said the Spanish Vice-Consul in Marseilles, "we know that the Poles are a warlike, adventurous nation. The war in Europe is over, as Hitler will be in London on August 15th. No wonder that the Poles want to leave Europe when there is no more fighting there. They heard about a good war in China, still going strong, and they want to enlist there. . . . Perfectly natural thing for the Poles to do."

The Poles were modest enough not to contradict. They did not mention the fact that they would be glad enough to stay at home if it was their own. They just grabbed every conceivable kind of visa and trekked towards a country which was as yet completely strange to them, but which was the only one to continue the struggle against Hitler.

After landing, they had a good look round. There was grass, more luscious and green than any they had seen in France, fed by the rich moisture of the ocean. The houses seemed mellowed by age, perhaps slightly stained by the smoke of the cities. The people were quiet, reserved, steady. They kept smiling, even when there was little reason for good humour, and it was difficult to read on their faces the news of the day. They went on with their work in the hard days of the late summer of 1940, apparently unaffected, stubborn, relentless and purposeful.

"This front won't crack," said Corporal Gruda, three days after their arrival in Glasgow.

The news was heartening, for the authority of Corporal Gruda stood high. He was a veteran of the last war and was known to be wary in his appreciations. He was a shrewder judge of the moral credit of nations than some wizards of the City and many a country completely failed to win his approval. After three days of careful consideration, his verdict was made.

"You mind my word, boys. This front will hold. They

won't crack. It's not easy to get to know them, but when one does, it's going to last. We won't go from here to any America or Canada, but just back home with those fellows."

Sceptical minds, inclined to query even the most authoritative pronouncements, wondered how the Corporal managed to get to know the British. His foreign vocabulary was known to be somewhat limited and its English section practically non-existent.

The great man sensed the unspoken doubt of his critics. " One gets to know them in a bar of theirs, drinking that yellow vodka. They slap you on the back and you slap them. They laugh and you laugh. When they say ' No,' you say ' No,' too. When they say ' Yes,' all you've got to do is to say ' Yes.' The booze is all right ; kind of herb vodka. Of course, it's not like our czysta, but it's a man's drink all the same. I like it better than that Calvados they brew from apples in France. You should learn English, my lads. Vodka is called whisky ; remember—whisky. Or better still—large whisky."

Such was the Polish soldiers' first acquaintance with the language of Shakespeare.

Chapter 3

TWO STRANGERS

SCOTLAND has known no invasion for many centuries. The Romans never reached it ; William the Conqueror landed on a distant coast and Scotland remained herself. But such inviolability could not remain permanent. The peaceful Polish invasion came as a terrible blow. The news spread like fire, from Glasgow and Edinburgh to Perth, St. Andrews, Dundee, Forfar and Inverness. Scottish children had heard a good deal about Redskins, Chinamen, Negroes and Eskimos, and about many other races and nations. They even knew the Hebrews and the Egyptians from their Scripture and the Assyrians and Phoenicians from their lessons. But they knew nothing about the Poles. A new migration of nations was needed to help them make their acquaintance.

" And where do the Poles live ? "

" In Poland."

This was hardly helpful.

" And what language do they speak ? "

" Polish," replied someone particularly well informed.

" Really ? They speak Polish ? " wondered the listeners. And they gasped before the vastness of the world and the number of tongues brought about by the silly notions of the architects of Babel.

" What does one eat in Poland ? "

" Bread, meat," answered the first Pole to be questioned.

The reply seemed to strike everyone as quite unexpected and stirred their interest in the mysterious country.

" Ah, and have you got trams ? "

" Yes."

" And fireplaces in the houses ? "

" Very few fireplaces."

This worried everyone and caused sympathy.

" Then how do you manage in the winter ? It is terribly cold there, isn't it ? "

" We make fire in the stoves," replied the Poles; " there are plenty of those."

General amazement.

" Do you have Christmas ? "

" Do you play golf ? "

" And tennis ? "

" How about fishing ? "

" Do you read the Bible ? "

" Do you get news from your people in Poland ? "

" How did you like Norway? It is very much like Poland, isn't it ? "

The Poles asked their own questions, stammering a good deal at first.

" So you are not English ? "

" No. Haven't we told you we are Scots ? "

" Then why do you speak English ? "

" We speak English, but we are Scotch. The Americans speak English, too, and the Canadians and the Australians. They are not English, but they do speak the language."

And they added : " When we win this war, you Poles will speak English, too. It's quite easy. . . ."

The Poles did not think it easy at all. But Scottish children made a game of singing Polish words aloud in the streets. They greeted every soldier with a choral of : *Dzien dobry* (good morning), *Dobry wieczor* (good evening), *Dowidzenia* (goodbye), *Czolem* (salute).

" A Polish soldier called me *paskudna*. What is *paskudna* ? " asked a fair maid of Perth.

" Well, perhaps you were not nice enough to that soldier," another Pole tried to explain.

" Oh, yes, I was very nice, indeed," said the girl, " but he expected too much sympathy for his country."

Old religious feuds, dormant for a long time, were

revived. " So the Poles are Catholics ? " asked a member of the Church of Rome, with keen interest.

" Of course. We are all Catholics."

" All of you ? Extraordinary."

The few Scottish Catholics were quite excited to hear about a country in which the whole population is Roman Catholic. The Sunday mass in the camps and the large numbers of Poles crowding into Catholic churches impressed them very much.

" Yes," they said; " you see, sometimes people tell us that Hitler is a Catholic, and the Italians, and they say that the Pope is too mild with the Axis. We are glad to have you here—now we can point to you and show them that the Catholics are the first to fight against Hitler."

The first canteens for the Polish troops were organised by the kind and helpful Church of Scotland organisation. The Poles, remembering the good work of the Y.M.C.A., went there in numbers, incurring the disapproval of their Scottish co-religionists, who were quite worried.

" How can you go there ? " they asked with horror. " Don't you see ' Church of Scotland ' written even on the plates and napkins ? They are dissenters, heretics really. They are sure to convert you. Are you going to part with your faith for a mess of pottage ? "

" There is no conversion about it," replied the Poles. " They just talk and talk and we eat. They are very kind and nice. We would rather have such ·Protestants than some German Catholics. Besides, we don't even under-stand what they are talking about, so how do you expect them to convert us ? And they never serve *potage*; it's mostly cocoa."

The adage about the sale of birthright was taken rather literally by the Poles, not so well read in Scripture as their Scottish Catholic friends, who still nursed some anxiety for the souls of their Polish brethren in the Church, exposed to the full blast of Protestant persuasion in the seductive atmosphere of the canteens. But the Church of Scotland was pleased to see hundreds of Catholics eating its fish and chips, with Horlick's or tea.

" We have never yet attracted so many Catholics," they said with satisfaction. " The Poles are clearly not fanatics, and Popery has not yet got a real grip on them. They may still see the truth."

" It's a lovely canteen," the soldiers told each other ; " clean, well-served, cheap. Everyone is very polite. What can those Catholics want with them ? They are very nice people, the Church of Scotland. If only they had some real drinks, it would be perfect."

Chapter 4
SOLDIERS TURN INTO AN ARMY

ONE of the largest initial camps of the Polish army in Scotland was lodged in the huge park of a magnificent Stuart mansion. There were old oak trees and various ponds and lakes, in a pattern reminiscent of an eighteenth-century etching. The beautiful, rich green lawn served as a carpet in the tents.

" You still pitch tents sometimes in Poland, don't you ? " asked the descendants of the Picts, reluctant to abandon the idea of a strange and exotic Poland.

The more enterprising soldiers started fishing in the ponds and setting rabbit traps in the park. " You mustn't," said the commandant of the Polish camp ; " no fishing, no poaching on Allied territory."

Some weeks later the British authorities found out that there were too many rabbits and that they did a lot of damage in the fields. Special announcements were posted in every town and village. " Rabbits are a dangerous pest and should be destroyed by trapping, shooting or other means. By catching a rabbit you contribute to victory."

The talents of the Polish peasants, born poachers, came in useful and from them many village lads learnt well-tried tricks.

" Did you set traps for the Germans at Narvik ? " they asked. The Poles understood only the word " Narvik," and replied with a significant " Yes, yes, Narvik—bum, bum."

" Narvik, bum, bum," was a fairly accurate description of the campaign and impressed many younger listeners, as well as the fair sex, by its manly brevity. Sundry stories about Narvik were often a kind of cunning psychological trap for catching other game than rabbits.

Gradually, slowly, new formations were organised out of the mass of the survivors of the French disaster. The officers were segregated from the other ranks. Some of the older officers went away—to London—sighed lovers of metropolitan life.

Then the airmen were picked out. Everybody tried his best to leave the miserable crowd of infantry, condemned to a long wait, and join the marvellous Air Force. Unfortunately, it was rather more difficult than finding pretty girls and hunting rabbits.

Then red tape, spun tirelessly by scores of staff men and small regimental scribblers, began to wind its way round and round everybody until they were entangled in a mass of papers stating the maiden name of the mother, the birthplace of the father, the last domicile in Poland and many other things which seemed infinitely remote to the exiles in Scotland.

Finally the new units were fitted out and equipped. The French uniforms were replaced by British battledress. The change was unanimously admitted to be one for the better. British arms were issued to the soldiers instead of their French weapons.

" Oi ! " complained some of them, " I will have to learn everything about a rifle for the third time in my life. First it was a Polish, then a French and now a British one. There will be a lot of cleaning with this Lee Enfield and in this damp climate things get rusty overnight."

The lieutenant heard it and immediately asked for double rations of grease, adding three hours to the time destined for rifle cleaning. It was the old army life again.

* * *

Autumn was approaching. It was to be their first autumn since the September of 1939.

In Poland autumn is the finest season, the best time of the year. It lasts from the end of August until the middle of November. There are many weeks of beautiful sunny weather without excessive heat. The autumn of 1939 had been one of the finest for several years ; the German armoured divisions had moved easily across dry fields and low-running rivers.

It was their first autumn in exile and their first autumn in Scotland.

The hills turned fawn and brown with the glow of the reddening leaves, bracken and heather. The trees in the park began to shed their yellow leaves. The harvest was over and the plough turned up the earth, sometimes lean with gravel and sometimes dark and heavy, just like the earth of Poland used to be. The sky grew somewhat darker and deeper, with brighter stars than before. At night, when soldiers kept guard at the camp, they often looked at the stars, for they were exactly like those they had seen in Poland on dark, frosty nights.

Damp nights and rainy days are dangerous not for rifle barrels alone. Souls get rusty, too, without the ointment of good news from home, of a kind word, of family warmth and friendly feeling. They get rusty if the trees along a road never look like those of the home village, if the children you meet in the street don't laugh and smile at you with the same confidence as there, and if the girls don't return your look as they did before. And if the sky is never the same as it was in Poland.

Chapter 5

VIRTUTI MILITARI

IT'S an unexpectedly sunny day in a small Scottish town, full of troops and animated by the festive occasion. In the square there is a dais with British and Polish colours. It's the Polish soldiers' day and the Commander-in-Chief is to be there.

The Scottish public was to see on parade for the first time the army which it already knew as its guest. The soldiers looked quite different from their private, shy, rather embarrassed selves trying to speak English with very few words and no accent at all.

They marched past with martial step, in perfect timing. Here comes the Podhale Brigade, of Narvik fame. They wear broad capes thrown back on the shoulders ; soldiers seasoned in the battles of Norway and France.

Here is the cavalry, with rifles slung on their backs, as they used to wear them in Poland, when riding on horseback. In a few months' time they are to get tanks and armoured cars instead.

And this is the unit which is most popular with the local public. It is a battalion with badges bearing the arms of Scotland on their helmets and the Stuart tartan for their regimental colours. When they return to Poland and develop into a full regiment again, the tartan will remain, a memory of Scottish hospitality and friendship. They march past General Sikorski, who reviews his army, accompanied by British and Polish guests. It is in many ways " his army." Did not its members cross many frontiers to come to France, in answer to his appeal ? Did they not follow him to Britain when France collapsed ? Now, under his orders, they are training in the use of the new weapons given them, ready to go into battle again when the time comes.

* *
*

On a green and gently sloping field, framed on each side by forest, the different units took up their positions, in close formation. General Sikorski, with his staff, walked along the line of the troops, while the band played the national anthem.

The standard of the Podhale Brigade, the one from Norway, bowed down before the Commander-in-Chief. On it General Sikorski tied the rustling blue and black ribbon of the highest Polish military decoration, " Virtuti Militari," and said, " For Narvik."

Then he decorated soldiers with Virtuti Militari and the Cross for Valour. For Narvik.

A blind soldier, who lost his sight at Ankenes, received from the Commander-in-Chief the highest honour— Virtuti Militari.

The Polish boy-scout, Casimir Dziedzioch, who smashed two German machine-gun nests with his hand grenades at Ankenes and lost a leg on his seventeenth birthday— Virtuti Militari.

And then they read the roll call of those left in the silent, grey, stony cemetery of Narvik. They received their reward on a sunny Scottish meadow, crowded with people. It was—Virtuti Militari.

Chapter 6

INTER-ALLIED STUDIES

" THIS Cadet will report to-morrow for duty," said the Aide-de-Camp.

" Oh, yes," answered the Colonel, " why are they sending him down here from Edinburgh ? What's the idea ? "

The Aide-de-Camp kept silent for a moment, long enough to dissociate himself discreetly from the opinion of his chief.

" We did want an interpreter."

" So we did, but why not send an officer, or else a simple private ? He would serve as telephone operator. The Major might be able to get along with his French. . . ."

The Aide-de-Camp thought that the Major's French was rather like the British liaison officer's Polish—mostly made up of good intentions. He gently reminded the Colonel of that fact.

" Oh, it's all right," said the Colonel, " let him come if he must. Who is he, anyway ? Probably a reserve man ? "

" He is."

" He would be," moaned the Colonel in a tone of a bitter ' I told you so.'

The Aide-de-Camp was non-committal and merely smiled. The Major, who had just walked in, listened in silence.

" And what else ? " asked the Colonel, gloomily.

" He is a doctor——"

" Send him to the first-aid station," brightly suggested the Major.

The Aide-de-Camp went on, " . . . of law and philosophy."

" Of law and philosophy," repeated the Colonel.

" Of law and philosophy," repeated the Major, in the same voice. They looked at each other understandingly.

" One has to be prepared for anything in wartime."

Only the General, on his return from inspection, took a more cheerful view of the situation.

" It's exactly what we wanted. He knows English; he was at Oxford, a scholar and lawyer; he will be able to tell us a great deal about Britain and British life. Yes, gentlemen. You play cards, you go shooting and you enjoy yourselves in town, wasting a lot of time. We should get to know our Ally better."

When the new Cadet reported for duty on the following day, the General said : " I've heard about you. We have plenty of time in the evenings and my officers are very sorry to have to waste it on nothing. They feel that they have no opportunity for learning and for the improvement of mind, which they would appreciate so much. Of course, at their age they probably won't be able to learn the language ; at any rate, not well enough to read anything less thrilling than Edgar Wallace. I hope you may help. . . ."

" Yes, sir."

" Well, you might perhaps tell us something in the evenings. You know, about everything. . . . You see what I mean. . . . We might start to-night after dinner . . . yes, at nine. . . . ."

* * *

Unpacking his very small bag in the garret in which he was billeted, the Cadet was wondering what information he would be required to provide for his superior officers. He was not at all sure that he could reply to some of the more complex questions which he anticipated. Would it be something about English literature and art ? Perhaps the status of the Empire and the main lines of British policy ? It might be the problem of peace aims, of the effectiveness of the blockade, or of a counterplan to Hitler's

" New Order." He felt that he would have to keep his wits about him if he was not to disgrace Oxford at staff head-quarters. He looked forward to the evening with interest, rather as to a *viva voce* on an unknown subject.

The General could not miss such a splendid opportunity for a little speech of about half an hour.

" Gentlemen," he said, among other things, " I am glad that I have found at last some means to help you in your study of British conditions. I know how hard you have tried to learn and what obstacles you have encountered. This Cadet, who has taken more degrees than we have received promotions, is willing to assist you in your difficulties and place at your disposal his knowledge of this country. I am sure you will all welcome this oppor-tunity of throwing new light on problems in which you have been interested for a long time. I know how eager you are to know Britain and I have no doubt that your desire for knowledge and information will be satisfied."

Thus the General concluded his little introductory speech. The Cadet sat modestly on the edge of a chair. A group of senior officers, deep in their armchairs, listened to the orator in a mournful silence, dreaming of the lost paradise of the daily game of poker.

" And now ask questions, gentlemen, ask questions ! " the General urged them on as he would horses in front of a broad ditch.

No one wanted to jump first. There seemed to be a conspiracy of silence. After many months of meditation on various subjects, nobody dared enter the " Open Sesame " of knowledge.

" Forward, gentlemen — courage ! " persuaded the General, as though they were about to enter a lion's den alone. " You should not hesitate to ask any question. Let everyone come forward with whatever interests him most. You seem to have something on your mind, Colonel ? "

" Well," said the Colonel, realising that the weight of

senior rank and its responsibilities is sometimes a heavy burden, " I would like to learn something about those— well, about the drinks they've got here. The wines they drink. Or take their whisky ; one drinks it day after day and knows nothing about it. I don't like to be so ignorant."

" That is splendid "—the General was always the first to give due credit for courage in the field—" you just have to speak frankly about the subject you are most interested in. I don't think many of you care about their painting or the views of those Socialist fellows. It would be no fit matter for officers. Hunting etiquette, something about golf, about drinks and about club rules—this is the knowledge which a Polish officer should bring back with him from the West. Let no one say that we wasted our time in Britain."

He turned to the slightly surprised Cadet. " Well, my dear fellow, what can you tell us about the British beverages ? What about sherry, port and, first of all, what about whisky ? "

" And what did they drink in the past ? " added the Padre, who has always had a historical turn of mind.

" What could they have drunk ? " objected the Major, regarding such intellectual speculation as quite irrelevant; " the same as we did. We drank vodka and they drank whisky. It has always been so and always will be."

* * *

" Not quite," said the Cadet; " if you don't mind, I will tell you about the evolution of drinking in the countries of the Red Lion and of the White Eagle. . . ."

" Very good. That is the real scientific approach "— the General commended his effort—" at last we shall know which king introduced his subjects to whisky and which taught his nation how to take down a swig of vodka."

" In the early period of the history of England and Scotland, as well as that of Poland, there was no wine, while vodka and whisky were unknown. . . ."

" Then how did they live ? "   The Major seemed sorry for his ancestors.

" Perhaps they did have something," suggested the Colonel, trying to be more optimistic, " only it was eventually forgotten ? "

" Nothing of the sort ! " went on the Cadet; " there is no doubt on the subject, because the contemporary chroniclers described banquets with as much gusto as they did battles, and we have very accurate accounts of the manner in which the King of Poland, Boleslaw Chrobry, entertained Otto, Emperor of Germany, in the year 1000. There are also records of the menus of the early mediaeval rulers of Scotland. The laborious monks missed nothing."

" That reminds me," broke in the General, " I just wanted to ask the Padre to write a history of our brigade from the day of landing in this country. History certainly has its uses. . . ."

" The beverages of early England and Scotland were something like half-fermented beers and ciders. Beer was also known in mediaeval Poland, according to German historians of the eleventh century. But the favourite drink of the Poles of that time was honey mead, almost unknown elsewhere. Fermented mead acquired after a few years extraordinary strength. It affected the legs more than the head, so that after a few glasses one could not get up, let alone walk. The exact date of the first appearance of whisky is unknown. Its Celtic name suggests very ancient origin, but the matter remains somewhat obscure. As to wine, the habit of wine drinking was introduced in Britain much later, as a consequence of the growth of overseas trade. Political reasons also played an important part. . . ."

" What have politics to do with it ? " asked the General.

" The English kings of the thirteenth and fourteenth centuries were also the suzerains of great French duchies, like Normandy, Languedoc, Gascogne and others. They were influenced by the culture of rich France and brought

French wines to England. If it wasn't for Joan of Arc the English would probably never have heard of sherry or port, but would still be drinking Armagnac, Bourgogne and Anjou. . . ."

" Joan of Arc ? " The Padre pricked up his ears.

" It was the misfortune of French wines, French culture and possibly European peace that the English were driven out of France by that saintly but somewhat shortsighted woman. . . ."

" Sir. . . ."

" The boy is right "—the General cut short the Padre—" for the result is that Hitler is in Paris to-day."

" A hundred years later it looked very much as though Spanish wines were to come to Britain for good. The Crown Prince of Spain, later Philip II, was the husband of Queen Mary, and if the invasion attempted by the Great Armada had succeeded it is likely that the popularity of Southern Xerez, that is sherry, would have increased very considerably. But wars against Spain and France were an obstacle to the peaceful penetration of Spanish and French wines into English stomachs. Portugal won the battle. As you certainly know, this small country, unlike Spain and France, has been for many centuries a staunch ally of England. By the treaty of friendship of 1704 the Lisbon Government abolished duty on English cloth and the London Customs admitted Portuguese wines duty free. There was a tremendous drop in their price. It was a real revolution—mostly in favour of the wines of the Porto region, sweet to suit mediaeval taste and strengthened by adding grape alcohol during fermentation. A glass or a bottle of port after dinner became a habit, and after about a century of such faithful attachment to allied drinks, gout was well on the way to becoming the fashionable, national complaint. It was just the same thing in contemporary Poland. . . ."

" In Poland, too ? "

" Yes. The country was becoming more prosperous

towards the end of the Middle Ages, and close relations with Hungary and Bohemia encouraged the use of wine. They were at first mostly light Bohemian and Polish wines, from vineyards established by the monastic orders. . . ."

" We have always owed culture to the Church," said the Padre..

" And wine as well," the Major consented.

" But very soon the Hungarian wines of the Tokay region acquired a semi-monopoly, thanks to the proximity of Hungary and the friendly relations existing between that country and Poland. Already in the sixteenth century the Polish gentry made good use of its parliamentary representation, making the import of wine free of duty a privilege of the nobility. As you see, they were well ahead of the English."

" Parliaments have their uses after all," observed the Colonel.

" King Ladislas IV of Poland, contemporary of Charles I, suffered from gout, as well as his father, brother and many notables of the period. His ailment may have hindered him from carrying out the plans for the expansion of the Polish Navy.

" And what happened to honey mead ? " asked the General, anxiously.

" Mead, the ancient beverage of the Poles and other Slavs, was largely superseded by Hungarian wine. It remained, however, very popular until the end of the eighteenth century. The gradual disappearance of the huge forests, with their swarms of bees kept in hollow tree trunks, has contributed to its decline. In the seventeenth century Poles got drunk on mead and wine. In the eighteenth French influence introduced wines from France as a high-class beverage. Champagne was just becoming the fashion. But the conservative squires believed to the end that the true Pole should drink only Hungarian wine and wear the national dress, instead of looking for champagne and adopting the ridiculous knee-breeches and wigs.

Beer was altogether in the background. It was used mostly in the form of the traditional Polish soup of hot beer with cheese. . . ."

" So beer is an old drink in Poland ? "

" As old as the Slavs. Beer, which is nowadays regarded as a typically German beverage, was taken by the Germans, together with some other things, from the Western Slavs. This was at the time when Berlin was a Slav village."

" So the Poles knew beer before the Germans ? "

" They did. It seems that they valued it very highly, if we are to believe the testimony of historians. One of the Popes, I now forget which, relieved the Poles from the duty of participating in a crusade. The Poles argued that they had been informed from trustworthy sources that beer could be taken only as far as Cyprus, after which it turned sour. This rendered any military action beyond that island quite impossible. His Holiness admitted the argument as perfectly valid and absolved the Polish knights from crusading on this occasion. . . ."

" And there are still people who say that the Holy See has no understanding for national interests ! " the Padre exclaimed.

" . . . and so the Poles did not go to the Holy Land, apart from a few exceptionally pious knights, who also happened to prefer wine to beer. But beer remained for a long time a strong favourite with the Poles. In the fifteenth century one of the Piast Princes of Silesia, Conrad of Gniewkow, received from the Pope the rank of Archbishop of Salzburg. It was a marvellous opportunity, for the Duchy of Gniewkow was a small one and the seat of Salzburg highly prized. Prince Conrad went as far as Vienna, but when he learned there that there was no beer in Salzburg and that it could hardly be brewed there on account of a shortage of barley, he returned to the Pope his emblems of office and went back to his poor Duchy, where he soon died. . . ."

" Probably D.T.," said the Major, knowledgeably.

" The hand of the Lord reached him," declared the Padre.

" It's all very well, my dear fellow, but when did vodka first appear in Poland ? "

" Spirits under the name of *aquavita*, *gorzalka* and others were in use from the beginning of the modern era. They were strong, but impure, and their use was mostly confined to the lower classes. It was alcohol distilled from rye. In the beginning of the nineteenth century potâtoes began to be used for this purpose and the barley vodka was much better than before. When the partitions brought with them Custom tariffs and an increase in the price of Hungarian and French wines, vodka became popular and soon won world fame, thanks to the practical publicity given it by the Russians. Such is the story of drinking in our two now Allied Countries."

" Thank you very much," said the General; " your interesting talk proves conclusively the value of international alliances and their beneficial results. Why, if it was not for the treaty with Portugal we would not be drinking port to-day, and, without our friendship with Hungary, Poland might have never tasted Tokay. Yes, gentlemen, history leaves a mark on our lives. May the new friendship between Poland and Scotland open our country to the salutary influence of whisky." And he drained his tumbler of Scotch.

Chapter 7

LOVE AND THEOLOGY

THE big temporary camps were gradually emptying. The soldiers were absorbed into the new units and the new army was taking shape. The huge park with its old trees and Jacobean castle was silent again. The new Polish camps were scattered all over Scotland, in small towns and villages. When they had to leave their first billets, the soldiers realised again the truth of the old Polish cavalry song :

> Soldiers, soldiers, lovely lads
> Many a girl will follow
> And maybe many a widow.

The Scottish girls proved to be the best teachers of English. Even the laziest pupils made remarkable progress. Soon after arriving at their new quarters the men asked for one or two days' leave, fully appreciative of that British institution, the week-end. " Where do you want to go ? " asked the officer.

" To where we camped before, to see our pals."

The Commander smiled and ordered the Sergeant to write out a furlough. Then he observed casually : " You know that camp there has been wound up, so you are not likely to find your pals there."

But this would not discourage the man at all.

" I will go there all the same, sir. Nice country, good to look at. . . ."

" You spent four weeks looking at it," said the Lieutenant, " but if you want some more, go there. Mind to be back in time."

The week-ends were not wasted.

"Do you know that the Sergeant who was with us in Dundee got married last Sunday?"

"Did he?"

"Yes, indeed. Kowalski was at the wedding. She is a pretty blonde, a Dundee girl, too. . . ."

The rains had come and water dripped steadily through the roof of the attic in the farmhouse in which they were billeted. But a long conference was held at night, before falling asleep, on the subject of the first Polish-Scottish marriage.

"It isn't the first; there have been two marriages already in the Armoured Brigade."

"They always get in first," grumbled the infantry, inclined to envy the speed of penetration of the armoured units. "Now when they got the black shoulder straps, they swagger about as though they had won about three wars."

"What will the Padre have to say about it?" someone enquired.

The Chaplain, a man of stern principles, had just incurred the resentment of his military flock. He succeeded in casting a chill on the delicate flower of Polish-Scottish friendship. Many girls who looked at the Polish soldiers at first with sentiments natural in a British maiden towards Allies oppressed by the Germans now turned their back and kept aloof.

"What on earth can have happened?" the soldiers wondered; "it must be the work of the Fifth Column."

A close investigation, probably assisted by a female Quisling among the enemy ranks, revealed the facts. The Padre was responsible for everything. He dared to bridge the chasm which has existed for centuries between the Churches of Scotland and of Rome, by going to the local minister and making a terrible confession:

"Our soldiers are after your girls, my reverend colleague."

"I gathered so," replied the Minister, "but I understand that they have matrimonial intentions. . . ."

"Don't you believe it," said the ruthless Padre, "I know my flock well enough. It's a flock of wolves rather than of lambs. They are not thinking of marriage at all, but they will do with your ewes as wolves have always done. They will leave them, they will . . . lucky if without a baby. . . ."

"Bless my soul!" moaned the Minister; and promptly warned his congregation of the danger. The girls promised to beware of the Poles as of the Evil One himself. They kept their promise faithfully—until the next dance.

"Well, what have you got to say now?" the soldiers triumphantly asked of the Padre; "aren't we to marry? Are we a lot of blasted Don Juans?"

The Chaplain went back to the Minister.

"My dear colleague, those rascals have started marrying. . . ."

"They have," replied the Parson sweetly. "I have just announced two more weddings. The boys are really not as bad as all that. They have serious intentions, which meet with the approval of the Church. . . ."

"Of the Church of Scotland, you mean," objected the Padre. "They all go through the Protestant ceremony, which . . ."

"The Church of Scotland is the Church of an Ally."

"I don't say anything to the contrary," puffed the Padre, "but they are lost to *the* Church."

"I am very sorry," the Minister continued, suavely; "perhaps my pious pupils showed them the real, I mean our, way to Salvation. If in the course of the war some Scottish troops are sent to Poland, they may marry in Catholic churches. It would be a kind of religious clearing arrangement. You have got very fine lads, Chaplain. They are not deaf to the voice of Faith coming from innocent Scottish maidens. They are willing to enter the path of search for Truth."

The Padre did not seem to share this view. Next Sunday he boomed from the pulpit : " You marry foreigners."

" They are Allies, Reverend Father."

" You will lose your nationality and your children will not be Poles."

" We shall teach our wives Polish."

" What will be left for the women of Poland ? "

" We will manage to have something left for them."

The preacher's words fell on a soil as stony as that of the Highlands. The Padre, reduced to concessions, made a last request :

" Promise at least that instead of talking nonsense to those girls you will convince them of the superiority of our Holy Faith over their heresy. Remind them of their blessed Queen Mary Stuart, who gave her life for the true Faith. You can turn a sinful meeting into a religious mission."

When he insisted, a few men promised to turn missionaries, but without great enthusiasm. Some of them even went so far as to mention Mary Queen of Scots when occasion permitted.

" Oh yes, I know "—the reaction was very promising— " I saw the picture. Garbo played Mary Stuart and Gary Cooper was her partner. No, I am wrong, it was not Gary Cooper, but a very handsome man just the same. No wonder the Queen went crazy over him. . . ."

The Mary Stuart gambit did not seem to work. Neither did the others. Their limited knowledge of English, as of theology, made such efforts rather difficult for the soldiers. In fact, they never even tried.

Chapter 8

THE GENERAL'S SUNDAY MEDITATIONS

"TELL me, gentlemen," said the General before the traditional Sunday bridge ; " tell me how to account for the popularity enjoyed by the Poles with the fair sex of this pleasant country. Perhaps you, Reverend Fathers, could throw a light on the subject ? "

Two Chaplains happened to be present and they took about a quarter of an hour exchanging courtesies and inviting each other to speak first. At last the General cut their quibble short and the elder of the two priests, who was, however, the junior in military rank, spoke on behalf of the Church :

" I think, General, that it is due to the Catholic spirit which our men radiate, not without calling forth a longing, quite natural among Protestants, to return. . . ."

" On the contrary," broke in his younger colleague from a cavalry regiment, " it seems likely that it is precisely the immoral side of the soldiers' character, alas, so often in evidence, that holds an attraction for women, who have always been known for their sinful inclinations. . . ."

But neither of the two theories was considered satisfactory. " Here is an example of a regrettable divergence of doctrine in a Church which calls itself universal," observed the General. " One of our spiritual guardians ascribes the phenomenon under review to the irresistible attraction of true faith and virtue ; the other, to the temptation of sinful ways. One holds that a vision of a lost Catholic paradise is all that the women can see in our boys ; the other, on the contrary, suggests that our men lead the local lassies, by way of cinemas and dance halls, in an altogether different direction. I am afraid that, unless we exclude the ecclesiastical element from this discussion, we are likely to witness the birth of a new Schismatic sect." He turned to the officers : " And what do you have to say ? "

" Money, sir ; it's merely money," said the Colonel, who intensely disliked any kind of discussion, especially a psychological one. " Our men have good pay. They can offer the girls an afternoon in a cinema, sweets and coffee. That's what women care for."

This view was not accepted by the General. " You are a complete materialist," he said ; " but your coarse materialism seems to be as far from the mark as the elevated spiritual motives mentioned by our Reverend Fathers. After all, the local young men certainly have at least as much money as our soldiers and probably far more. It isn't as though the Poles were millionaires in a country of paupers; quite the contrary. . . ."

And he turned to the Major.

" I think," said the Major, who had been dozing over his large whisky, " that the reason is not far to seek. It's the magic of the uniform. The local young men who are still available are mere civilians. Can you wonder that they stand no chance in competition with smart soldiers ? "

" Yes," said the Colonel, " but the soldiers of the English regiment stationed in C . . . are far from pleased with their romantic achievements. Their Colonel told me so yesterday."

" It's perhaps because, being British, they are not as exotic as a foreign army," argued the Major.

The General helped himself to some more whisky and nodded approval. " Very good, gentlemen," he said, " we are gradually approaching a solution of this intricate problem. We are agreed that it is neither Catholic virtue, nor the temptations of evil that are responsible for the popularity of our soldiers with the lassies of Scotland. We also ruled out the base materialist motives, so skilfully advocated by the Major. . . ."

" Excuse me, by the Colonel," the Major corrected.

" . . . Yes, by the Colonel, as inadequate to account for the phenomena under review. After all, a Scot can spend on a girl as much or more, and he is likely to know her better. And yet there is no doubt that our men are popular with the ladies. You have read, no doubt, in the British press, amusing stories about Englishmen pretending that they are Poles to win the favours of a Scottish girl. I confess that I can't see why they should resort to such a ruse—the British soldiers we see here are splendid, fine-looking lads. But, of course, no one can understand the whims of women. . . ."

" That's true," said the Major, who had recently returned from his leave in Edinburgh, gloomy and angry for no obvious reason.

" It's all true," went on the General ; " and we are certainly drawing nearer and nearer to the crux of the whole matter. But not far from K . . . there is a Norwegian camp, and I can tell you that our fellows are sometimes quite embarrassed to see how our dear Allies, in spite of their undoubted merit. . . . In T . . . there are some Czechs. They are getting on a little better, not so bad at all, but it's still nothing to compare with our chaps. The Poles are certainly first in this hurdle race, the Czechs poor seconds, and then there is simply nobody for a long way. Oh ! if this was a way of winning the war. . . . It's a curious fact and it still remains rather a mystery."

" They don't know us yet." Said in a sinister tone by the Chaplain, who a moment before had been crediting the Poles with conspiring with the powers of hell.

" Nor did they know us, my Reverend Father. They did not know us in July or August, but by December they must know about the worst. I suppose some of the natives, especially the women, might be able to tell the Padre some quite exciting details about the wickedness of his little flock."

The conversation would probably have remained confined to the General's taunts at the two representatives of the Church if it was not for the arrival of the learned Cadet, in company with the owner of the house, who, at the General's invitation, frequently joined the officers at their evening whisky.

"Here comes our answer," said the General. "He, as a native of the land, will be able to explain why the sedate Poles, as soon as they arrived on the shores of Loch Lomond, acquired the reputation of irresistible Don Juans."

After the time-honoured opening of the conversation with polite inquiries about health and "How do you like Scotland?" everybody settled down with their whiskies, and there would have been peace but for the General's restless curiosity.

"Ask him," he told the Cadet. "Explain to him the whole matter and tell him that I want to know, because a General must know everything about his men. Let him tell us why the Poles enjoy such an undeserved popularity with the girls of this country. What is the real reason?"

The Cadet took a long time explaining everything to the Scot, who listened patiently to a detailed account of the General's doubts and guesses. Then he asked again why the information was needed, and nodded on being told that it was merely a matter of psychological study. He took a gulp of whisky, poured himself some more and then said two very short words. The Cadet seemed embarrassed. The officers, blissfully ignorant of the language, continued their siesta.

"What did the Scot say?" asked the General, noticing the interpreter's uneasiness.

"Well, what was it?" insisted the Colonel, growing suspicious.

"He said," stammered the Cadet under pressure— "he said that it's because they are such good liars. No one in these parts can lie as they can. . . ."

" What ? " roared the Colonel.

" What do you mean ? " asked the Major, roused from his slumber.

" Are they liars ? " wailed the Padre, who a few minutes earlier had spoken of his pupils as true sons of the Devil. " They—liars ? Our Catholic soldiers, our Polish boys— liars ? "

" Be calm, gentlemen," said the General. " After all, it may be true. Ask him." He turned to the Cadet : " What does he exactly mean by being liars. Let him explain. We shall see. In the meantime, gentlemen, control your feelings. This promises to be most interesting."

The Cadet interpreted to the host the General's inquiry. The Scot puffed his pipe pensively and was lost for a while in deep meditation. After a few minutes he cleared his throat and began talking at great length to the Cadet, stopping from time to time.

" He has never been so talkative yet," observed the Colonel.

" He is always like that on Sundays," explained the Padre ; it is the refreshing effect which Bible reading has on the mind."

" It's more likely due to the fact that on week-days he doesn't sit down to whisky until the evening, and on Sundays he gets to it early in the afternoon," said the sceptical Padre from the Lancers regiment.

" Reading the Bible has a salutary effect on the mind and whisky has it on the body." The General offered an acceptable compromise and drained his tumbler to prove his words by action. " Let us see what the graduate of the two Universities will have to tell us about it."

The Doctor of Law and Philosophy listened carefully to the long argument of the Scotsman and then said :

" Gentlemen ! Our courteous host had no intention of passing unfavourable comment on our national character. His observation was somewhat paradoxical. But he has certainly provided an explanation of the puzzling phenomenon. He told me why the Poles enjoy a greater popularity with the ladies in Scotland than they did in Rumania, Norway or in France. . . ."

" It was not so bad in France," protested the Major.

" Nothing to complain about in Rumania," added the Colonel.

" I was told by others," said the Padre, " that in Norway . . ."

" You are quite wrong," said the General, " and you should not boast. It is not done. What I am interested in is the fine sentiment which we find here and which was absent there."

" Shall I translate our host's account for you ? " asked the Cadet. " Of course, it's a fairly long story."

" Yes, tell us all about it," said the General ; " it is Sunday, and those gentlemen will do well to give some thought to something serious."

The Cadet opened a new bottle of Black and White and filled everybody's glasses. The host, deep in his armchair, seemed to enjoy listening to the voice of the young Pole, his interpreter.

Dissertation about the Lie in Love, or the Reasons for the Popularity of the Polish Soldiers in Scotland

" Well, gentlemen, the Poles are liars.

" The Briton regards the lie as a disgusting and revolting crime, little better than robbery, burglary or rape. Of course, there are liars in this country, but they lie for base and shameful reasons ; for instance, in order to avoid well-deserved punishment or jail.

" Those cold northern countries are ruled by the severe law of the Scandinavian sagas and the stern code of the Old Testament, which ruthlessly punished the lies of Eve and of Cain, of Joseph's brothers and of Potiphar's unfaithful wife. It is to be observed that, whenever some lying occurs in the sagas or in the Old Testament, there is some very shady motive behind it—murder, treason, cowardice or something equally despicable. The northern nations, bred in the tradition of the sagas and fed every Sunday for centuries on severe Old Testament, developed a holy fear of untruth and learned to avoid it as much as crime itself. They knew no other lies than those of sinister wrongdoers.

" Things took quite a different turn with the Poles. The Scandinavian sagas reached the banks of the Vistula in a somewhat distorted and rather comic form; as for instance, the story about the king who was eaten by mice. Catholicism replaced the gloomy accounts of the misdeeds of the early Hebrews with colourful and human stories about the lives of the saints. The mild character of the Slavs softened everything with which it came into contact. Finally the Latin, Mediterranean, Hellene and Gallic influences brought with them the lessons of Ovid, who advised the embellishment of love with lies, of Petrarca, who offered his mistress flowery untruths, and of Ronsard, who lulled his love with sweet flattery. Eventually the Poles learned, too, to speak of love. What is even more important, they learned how to be good liars in love."

" Do you mean to say," the Major exclaimed, " that the British never speak about love at all ? "

" They don't. They look upon it as improper, immoral and even unmanly. If they do speak about it, they get over it as quickly as they can. They try to avoid big words, promises and declarations, or at least ration them to an absolute minimum."

" Well, then," said the Colonel, quite puzzled, " how on earth do they get along with women ? "

" They use all the other methods. They look at a girl, try to meet her, to see her whenever possible. They call on her, but part of the visit may be spent reading newspapers or smoking a pipe. If the girl seems to take it well, things get along by roundabout ways. A young fellow talks for a bit about his intention of settling down ; hints at a rise

he is expecting at New Year, and promises a ruby engage-
ment ring. The more daring speak about their love of
children. Any but the most brainless girl will soon guess
that the fellow is madly in love with her. But love itself is
jumped over, as something rather indecent. They probably
learn the leaping trick from salmon travelling upstream."

"As Northerners," announced the Colonel solemnly,
"they have no passions."

"On the contrary. They are perhaps more passionate
and vigorous in love than anyone else. But they are
ashamed of it. Their love has never basked in the warm
glow of southern roses or scarlet Polish poppies. It was
always hounded and chilled by the wrath of Puritan sermons,
as terrible as the Last Judgment. The voice of love was
hushed for fear of God. Anglo-Saxon affection had to find
for its expression undertones, whispers, delicate hints.
It was like painting in pastels instead of oils. . . ."

"Beautiful thing, the pastel. . . ."

"No doubt. Delicate feelings are beautiful, too. But
some people prefer gaudy colours and some are bored with
the maudlin tones of the pastel, thirsting for something
stronger and brighter."

"Or more eloquent."

"Yes. Sometimes the impenetrable defence wall, which
defied even the Romans, failed to stop a vague rumour
about other forms of love than those known to the fogbound
north. Strange tales were told about the seductive
Frenchmen ; the passionate Spaniards and the Italians
with their *grand'amore*. Even in the bleak north the dream
of another love flowered into the story of Tristan and
Iseult. . . ."

"Who are they?" asked the Major, to whom the
peculiar names were entirely new.

"Half a crown fine for every interruption," announced
the General.

"They are characters in a picture which is now showing
in Edinburgh," whispered the Colonel ; "only I forget

who is playing Iseult. See the film and you will know all about it. . . ."

" So people did hear from time to time about fairy princes, romantic knights and sublime love. For centuries the lovers and husbands of the women of Britain led the most romantic lives imaginable, sailing the oceans, discovering islands, subduing mutinies in India or inciting them in Arabia. They traded in wares as romantic as ebony and ivory, as precious as the pearls from the Gulf of Persia and the gold of Africa, as fragrant as the scents of the east and vanilla. But they were reluctant to tell about those marvellous adventures at home."

" Like true gentlemen," observed the Major.

" Half a crown," said the General impassively.

" Thus the life of their mates at home was laborious, domesticated, virtuous and dull. The country which dealt so severely with the Italian singer of Mary Stuart was not entirely unaware of the existence of another world, of other men and other loves. The cinema stirred imagination and feeling. It showed a new, glamorous and adventurous way of living ; women exciting violent passions and men condemned by the parson in his sermon, but glorified by their admirers and lifted to the state of legendary heroes of modern times. Men like Charles Boyer, Gary Cooper, Ramon Novarro, Tyrone Power, Clark Gable . . ."

" The Poles did not learn it at the pictures," corrected the Major.

" Another half crown," observed the General.

" Two decades and half the production of Hollywood were enough to produce more lovers and seducers than there are prophets in the Bible, not mentioning righteous men like Habakuk and distinguished leaders like Joshua. . . ."

" Joshua was not a prophet," admonished the Padre.

" You will pay half a crown, Reverend Father," said the General. " The next will pay five shillings."

" Every film was an erotic lesson surpassing the counsels

of Ovid or the sonnets of Petrarca. It was a practical demonstration of the most convincing kind. It impressed on women the fact that if a man is in love he should repeat the magic word as often as possible and gaze into her eyes for hours on end. He should be madly jealous, chivalrous and occasionally miserable. He should give her flowers and various trinkets. He should spend money freely and refuse her nothing. He should be tender, passionate and insistent. He should hold her in his arms and speak of love. . . ."

" I always said that the films . . ." exploded the Chaplain.

" One crown, please," said the General.

" And then, all of a sudden, Polish soldiers came quite unexpectedly to Scotland. They brought with them the charm of a country infinitely more exotic than India or Canada, which are, after all, not very far from Scotland. They had fought in Poland, in Norway and in France. Their country had suffered cruel martyrdom. They were soldiers ; they were Allies and they were guests.

But, first of all, they had different ways in love. The word " love " and others of the kind for them were not like a great ceremony, such as a wedding, which happens once in a lifetime, nor like something slightly indecent, that is best not mentioned. They were neither great nor indecent words. They were among the most common in the language. The foreign guests were lavish where the Englishman or Scotsman had been cautious and reserved. They were lavish with the wealth of words, simple and yet dear to every woman. To make it worse, the Poles did not have the reputation of libertines enjoyed by the French ; they were not associated with the dissolute Italians or Spaniards. They lived too far away; no one knew anything either good or bad about them, and the fact that they are a northern nation was rather in their favour. A Frenchman, Italian or Spaniard swearing eternal love might be the object of some well-founded suspicion, but not a Pole.

Didn't the press write a lot about the Poles being the most faithful Allies, true in time of misfortune ? "

" They are, as a nation . . ." observed the General.

" The natural inference was that a nation faithful in alliance and true to its honour would be composed of individuals of remarkable constancy. That is why the assurances of love made freely by the Poles were implicitly believed. When they told a girl that they loved her more than anyone else, more than anybody ever did or could love her, that she would be so loved for ever—why, there was not the slightest doubt left in her mind. The cinema prepared a receptive ground, and every woman wanted to taste once a grand passion, like those of the stars. The feminine mind has an organic need for masculine attention and affection. The well-worn words, hardly improved upon since the stone age, have retained most of their magic to this day. They are a narcotic enjoyed even by those who know its real value. Perhaps the wiles of the Poles were rather cheap and easy, but sometimes deception gives real pleasure and artificial jewellery or glamorous furs of domestic origin have great charm for those who wear them."

" All this is not very much to the credit of the Poles," said the Chaplain, sadly.

" Five shillings ! " The General cut him short.

" Perhaps it is to their discredit, perhaps not. Each country has its customs. They were trained to believe that only a deep sentiment can cause—h'm . . . justify a certain amount of aggressiveness towards women. They are used to the idea that marriage alone provides a moral form for certain manifestations of a social and sexual nature. The Church took good care to drive it all into their heads. That is why they now feel compelled to speak about eternal love even when their real motive is somewhat less elevated. That is why they speak about marriage even when all they want is a little flirt. . . ."

" That is treachery," said the Priest, sternly ; and the

General could not fine him, because he was just swallowing a glass of whisky at one gulp, Polish fashion.

" I don't know. Perhaps they do love at the moment when they speak about it and they do mean at the time their promises of marriage—which, by the way, are not infrequently kept. Their Slav nature is easily inflamed by feeling. The climate of their hearts seems as changeful as that of Scotland itself. They vary the objects of their affection, but it is nevertheless warm, passionate and genuine while it lasts. Calculated deception is alien to their character ; but they are earnest, absorbed and even violent in every one of their loves as though it was the first. This, apparently, makes an appeal in a country in which such expressions of passion are rather scarce. That is why the Scotsman ascribed their popularity to the fact that they are ' good liars.' The sweet words, the small attentions, flowers, flattery and unconcealed infatuation are for the Poles a cosmetic of love, no more meant to deceive than the lipstick on a girl's mouth. Are they liars ? Medicine knows drugs which are poisonous in large doses, but may be very helpful in small ones. Take arsenic. . . ."

" What you are saying now, my young fellow, is highly immoral."

" Not at all, Padre ; it's a perfectly accurate scientific analogy. A lie designed to cover the murder of a brother, like that of Cain, a robbery or some other serious misdeed was deemed as hideous as the crime itself, especially as it was inspired by a cowardly fear of punishment. But deception in love was merely an embellishment of certain feelings, their sublimation and expression in poetic terms. It's like a deadly poison turned into a fairly harmless drug with very pleasant effects . . . after all, those men don't live a joyful life; let them have at least that little. . . ."

" Have you finished ? " cautiously asked the Colonel, who had saved his shillings by keeping silent as a fish for the last half hour.

" Yes, I have."

" Well, I think that is not all.   The Poles, more than anyone in this country, are sensitive to-day to the attractions of a home, since their own homes are so far away.   They want womanly affection and softness, which is such a contrast after their two years of soldiering in the roughest conditions.   That is why they, like everyone else, and even more so, desire marriage and family life just now, when they are something remote and unattainable."

Everyone agreed and drank the health of the host.

" Thanks to you," said the General, " we have spent the afternoon in valuable psychological research.   The Major, I believe, will complete his studies in an Edinburgh cinema, as far as Tristan and Iseult are concerned.   The other gentlemen are requested to pay their fines.   The Padre pays most—three times five shillings plus half a crown: that is seventeen and six."

" I will pay, but you, sir, have also interrupted once, on the subject of national constance in alliances."

" If I did," said the General, " it was in the execution of my duty; but to set a good example, I will pay half a crown, too."

" Five shillings, sir.   You did it after raising the rate for interrupting the speaker."

Chapter 9

ON THE COAST

THE sandy dunes are old, so that the forest has had time to grow and grip the flimsy soil with its roots. The lanes are soft and many army lorries have to use all their gears to get through the more difficult parts.

On a square clearing there is a village of corrugated steel huts, rather like big barrels sliced into two and then placed with the open end on the ground. They also recall the hoods of gipsy waggons, as seen on nineteenth-century etchings. Everybody is glad to have exchanged canvas for iron, which rusts, but at least does not leak in the almost continuous autumn rain. The huts are dry inside, and on the beds, huddled in blankets, sleep those who came off duty at midday. They sleep soundly, although the radio—perhaps a gift of the Polish Relief Fund—is playing a merry tune and other soldiers are playing cards. Someone is reading.

The men keep guard on the coast. One follows the narrow lane through the forest, until it becomes a path. The sea is at that time of the year invariably misty and the moisture condenses in tiny droplets on the wool of great-coats, on the helmets and on the rifles, even when it is not raining. Everything is damp.

The sentries stop us again. They are British soldiers this time. They hold the next sector. A few hundred yards farther on we meet a Polish sentry and again the watchword is repeated. There are actually watchers who scan the grey sea, watching for anything out of the normal, watching incessantly through day and night. Many thousands of keen eyes are watching the sea along the whole length of the British coast.

It is always dark in the pillbox. There is a wooden table covered with a blanket. On the table there is some food. Round the walls there are benches on which one may sleep after sentry duty outside. If it was not for the penetrating, clammy cold, the 24-hours' watch would not have been much of a hardship. The day, and especially the night, would be shorter. But there is something weary and depressing about the sneaking cold and the dead silence of the dunes with their meagre pines. The roar of the waves and the whine of the wind do not break the silence, for they are themselves unbroken.

The men released from duty after their stretch of sea-watching are glad and walk off briskly, as though they were workmen leaving the factory for a home. They return to the pillbox and wait there until their next turn. The machine guns are ready, the observers are on the lookout, and everything relapses again into a frozen void. From time to time someone gets out and looks at the sea, only to return after finding that it has changed little in the last few hours, as little as in the last few thousands of years. There are minor differences. Sometimes the white-crested breakers hammer the beach angrily, and sometimes they seem to come in almost softly to land on the sloping sand like an aeroplane on a field. There are days when the horizon cuts a sharp boundary between the sea and the sky. But on most days there is a grey, misty no-man's-land between the sky and the sea, beginning a few hundred feet from the shore. It is also the no-man's-land between two worlds at war.

The dim light of the day dies out quickly. The candles stuck in an old tin provide scant illumination. Conversation, if any, is slow and sluggish. Even thought seems to switch into slow motion and the mind slacks down. Waiting for something that may never happen seems interminable. A sleepy brain chews the cud of very old or quite recent memories, almost inactive.

Those who have just returned stamp their feet loudly

on the floor, in an effort to strike a spark of warmth from the icy slabs of stone. One man is reading by the flickering light of the candle. Another, wrapped in blankets, is asleep. Two others wait in silence.

" What are you thinking about ? " one of them asked the other.

" Nothing in particular," he replied, still half-dazed ; " that is, just about everything. . . ."

Everything means home. It means some Miechow, some Srem, or Zamkowa Street in Wilno, Kleparow in Lwow. It means a family of whom there is no news. It means Poland.

" And what do you think about ? " he asked.

" Me ? Now about nothing. Before, I was thinking of Romek and Staszek."

A silence fell between them. Romek and Staszek were their friends from the same training company in France. They spent six months together. Then these two were detailed to the Third Division, still stationed in Brittany, and the others to the First Division at Sedan, and the Second on the Maginot Line respectively. Where are they ? Romek is probably a prisoner in Germany, or may be dead. Staszek is likely to be interned in Switzerland, idle.

" They say conditions in Switzerland are good. . . ."

" What's the use of good conditions if you can't do anything except wait and do nothing ? "

" Well, we are doing little else here, to tell the truth. We just patrol our sector, and watch the sea. . . ."

It is quite true. But the memory of those two who are God knows where contradicted his words. The other one felt it, too.

" It is not quite the same thing. We are, after all, the Polish Army. We survived September in Poland and June in France. We are still soldiers, and sooner or later we shall fight again. Would not Staszek and Romek like to exchange places with us in this cold pillbox, on a wintry

night ?   Or wouldn't our school-friends who remained in
Poland like to be here ?   Or those left in the Balkans, or
in France, or in German camps ?   They would love to
be where we are."

"Just think—this part of the Scottish coast has been
entrusted to us.   When we arrived we were really just a
crowd, debris of various units smashed in the Battle of
France.   Now we are a regular army.   It is true that some
of the regiments are staffed with officers only, waiting for
recruits from overseas, but there are many complete units.
Ours is at present the largest army of any Ally of Britain.
We still have a job of work to do."

"Do you think they will try to land here ? "

"Why not ?   They might try in many places at once.
It is quite likely that on a night like this one they will
come up under cover of darkness and fog.   Don't you think
they might slip through the net of the naval patrols and
get here ?   It is perfectly possible."

"Of course it is."

"We don't know when they will come.   It may be during
our watch.   It may be just afterwards, or to-morrow, or
four months later—or never.   The industry of Britain and
America is getting into its stride, but to get ahead of the
others we need time.   That is why we have got to hold out
until the arms are ready.   That is why we have to guard
this bit of coast as though it was Polish soil."

As the night grew darker, the wind was sharper and the
chill in the fog more piercing.   A tiny, obstinate little
light twinkled far away behind the trees.   Then it went
out.   Scotland was asleep.   The great cities and the
Highland villages slept.   Even the black-headed sheep
were asleep on their pastures.   Along the dented line of
the Scottish sea-coast the Polish soldiers are changing the
fourth watch.

Chapter 10

ENGLISH AND ITS CHARMS

THEY collected stray foreign words together with the dust of European roads, which clung to their boots. They learned that ' please ' in Serb is *molim*, and ' good-bye ' in Hungarian is *a viszontlátásra*—a bit of a mouthful even for Poles. In Rumania they called girls *domniszara* and flattered them with the word *fruma*, which means beautiful.

Then they started to study French and learned to call a girl mademoiselle and say *s'il vous plaît* for ' please.' Besides, many of them knew it already, for French has long been the universal language of love. In Norway they found out that a German is a *Tysk* and bread is *bred*. The simpler minds found considerable satisfaction in the fact that the Norwegian for ' fiord ' is exactly the same as the Polish *fiord*.

And then they had to start all over again. This time it was to be English.

Eight English teachers were assigned to the unit. They formed small groups of pupils and soon a monotonous choral was heard in the afternoons : the table ; the chair ; the bench ; the pencil ; the book. It is no easy matter to teach Poles to put their tongues in the correct position between the teeth, or wherever they have to be, to get the English ' the.' The whole group spent many hours trying to learn the trick, and drops of sweat stood out on some foreheads as they said for the hundredth time : ' Tze,' like so many buzzing bees. It was much harder work than the morning drill. Some dropped off, worn with exhaustion. Others carried gallantly on and repeated : yellow ; yellow.

" But don't say ' yellove '," said the teacher ; " it

should be just ' yellow.' You don't pronounce the ' w ' at the end. Say it again—' yellow '.'' They said it.

" Well, that's a lot better.'' The teacher seemed pleased with the result. " In another five or six years you will be able to speak English almost like Scots.''

The promise of years of sojourn in Scotland produced among the soldiers greater panic than news about the landing of ten thousand German parachutists would have done.

" I don't mean to say,'' the kind teacher explained, " that you will actually stay another five or six years. But I think that five years is the minimum period for learning the language of Shakespeare and Milton. Provided, of course, that you don't speak Polish among yourselves. . . .''

" But then, we will forget Polish, and when we finally do return home, we will be unable to talk to our wives, children or friends.''

" That will be splendid. You will teach them English. Now, please, repeat it once again : ' the pencil is blue ; the book is yellow.' ' Yellow '—not ' yellove.' Yes, that's better.''

The teacher is an old, retired schoolmaster, who volunteered for the work, like many other Scots. It reminds him of the times when he was teaching in a school. By helping Poles to learn English he is rendering to his country perhaps the last service he can offer at his age. He had never come across any Poles before. But he knows a little French and they know it, too. Sometimes, listening to someone reading the lesson—' wine is heavy, beer is light '—he looks through the window with his pale eyes, somewhere far away. Perhaps he is dreaming.

After the lesson he sometimes mutters, half to himself, " I wish you could read Shakespeare some day.''

But the soldiers are suspicious. " Is it poetry ? ''

" It is,'' replied the old teacher, " very fine poetry. Whole dramas.''

The soldiers looked at him in awed silence.

" Or if you could read Milton. That would be almost better. He wrote a long, wonderful poem," explained the teacher. " It is a great work, with deep religious meaning. . . ."

On the following day he brought a beautifully bound old volume, about the size of a Bible.

" This, dear boys, is Milton—a great British poet. You will be able to read him. And also Walter Scott, who wrote many novels and stories. And Shelley, another great poet. And Byron. And Keats. And . . ."

The terrified students were overwhelmed by the torrent of great names which they had recklessly unleashed by trying to learn the dangerous word ' yellow.'

" You see," continued the old schoolmaster, pleased to see the staggering impression which the greatness of English literature made on his pupils, " you are not learning English for nothing. All that and a lot more will be yours. On Sundays you will be able to sit quietly in a garden and read the Holy Scripture. It is extremely topical in wartime. Take, for instance, the story of David with his sling which killed the giant Goliath. It is obvious that Hitler is the modern Goliath. There is also the example of the ass's jaw-bone with which Samson defeated the wicked Philistines. . . ."

There was an atmosphere of gloom and foreboding during that day's lesson. The thought of Milton, Keats and the Bible had put the fear of God into everybody. The hazards of learning English were realised by all— too late.

* *

" What's the name of that fellow over there ? " the Captain asked the Lieutenant one evening at the entrance to the local cinema.

" It's Nowak, from the second platoon, sir."

" I see that it's Nowak, but what makes him so talkative ?

I wonder what language he is talking to the girl. Is she Polish ? I will have to find out."

The military machine was set in motion.

" Nowak," said the Lieutenant at the evening roll call, " who is the girl you were walking with in front of the cinema ? "

" The blonde ? "

" I don't care about the colour. It doesn't matter. What language were you talking ? Was it Polish ? "

" Nah, sir. What would be the good of talking Polish to her ? She's old Williams's daughter, of Edward Street."

" So what language did you speak, damn it all ? "

" English, sir."

The reply followed the well-worn channels of army bureaucracy and eventually reached the omniscient Captain.

" They talked English, sir."

" Don't tell me such nonsense," said the Captain. " Nowak does not know any language except Polish. I checked it in the records. Orderly ! Bring me here Private Nowak from the second platoon."

Private Nowak, summoned into the presence of his commanding officer, clicked heels in the approved manner.

" Ah, you ! So you know English, what ? Why didn't you say so when the records were made ? "

" What didn't I say ? "

" That you know foreign languages. You have been asked in July to put down everything for the records."

Private Nowak understood.

" In July I didn't know any English, but now, sir, I . . ."

" Now you know it, do you ? "

Nowak hesitated. " Well, I don't know it proper, sir, but I can get along. I did learn and read."

" What ? And you can talk with a girl ? "

Private Nowak grinned with a row of white teeth as dazzling as his boots, specially polished for the occasion.

" With a girl, sir, it's the easiest . . ."

" I know," said the Captain. " But you seemed to be

holding a regular lecture there, in front of the cinema. You were talking like a preacher."

"Well, sir, I was just telling her how we had to go home at Widze in sledges, across the frozen lakes. And in the summer one had to drive a long way round, so it was really much nearer in the winter. And I was telling her about driving in sledges, with bells, in deep snow. . . . And about fishing in those lakes. It was very difficult with the barbed wire left there by the Germans in the last war. They always tore the nets. But there was a lot of fish. And I told her other things about home. . . ."

The Captain looked at the Lieutenant, taking him for witness. "Do you hear it? He could tell her a long story like that." And then he turned to Nowak, who stood to attention, rather worried and wondering what to expect. "Dismissed."

Private Nowak went away, without knowing what sort of impression his attainments had produced. He was an old soldier and he knew that to be happy in the army one has to avoid the notice of all superiors and keep quiet about anything one may know. Back in his hut, he was still going over his interview with the Captain, rather uneasily. "Maybe it was a military secret about that barbed wire?" he reflected with a guilty feeling.

On the following day the Captain made a short speech in the morning. "You've been in this England, or what they call Scotland, for about four months and you're still as dumb as beasts. You are a disgrace to your country and to me, your commander. What idiots they are in that company, the natives here will say, that they only learned to say 'please' and nothing more. Instead of talking to a girl like smart fellows, with compliments and pretty words, some of you brutes start about it with your hands. That's all you know, stupid louts. I will give you extra potato-peeling, extra rifle-cleaning and fatigue duty unless you learn English properly in your spare time."

The company listened to the harangue in gloomy silence.

" Private Nowak ! "

" Present ! " cried the culprit loudly, bracing himself for the worst.

" Look at Private Nowak. Is he better than the others ? Is he more clever ? Not at all. But he obeys his Captain instead of twiddling his thumbs, and now he can speak English. He can tell his girl everything, not just a lot of nonsense. He can tell her about Poland. See what military discipline means ? Well, Nowak, you will be getting on all right ; just carry on."

He was about to leave, but he turned back : " Just a word, Nowak. It's all right about your learning English, but you were not in order, because you did not report it. As soon as you learnt the language, you should have gone to the Serjeant-Major and told him, so that it might be added to the records under your name, under : ' knowledge of foreign languages.' In the army every damned thing must be set down in the official records. And don't let the next ones forget it. You learnt a language—report to the Sergeant-Major. Make a note for the records. An army is an army. There must be discipline and order."

The company marched off for drill. The Captain, returning to his office with the Lieutenants, added : " Of course, it applies also to you, gentlemen. You should spend some time learning English properly. Do you want everybody in the ranks chattering as they like and the platoon commander dumb as a post ? "

" Damn Nowak and his girl," thought the Lieutenant, angrily. " What about the Captain's English ? "

The Captain seemed to have heard the unspoken remark. " I should have loved to do so myself. Ah, if I had only a platoon, not a whole company in my care ! And if I was younger ! "

He was exactly two years older than the Lieutenant.

***

The news about the remarkable linguistic attainments of Nowak delighted the old teacher.

"At last I have some real results," he told the less promising pupils. "Look at Nowak. It is true that he cannot pronounce properly either ' the ' or ' will,' or in fact anything at all, but you lazy fellows will still be learning ' A Thousand Words ' when he will be reading Milton and Shakespeare."

The class thought that Nowak would be likely to turn his newly acquired knowledge to an altogether different use, in the direction of the paradise of old Williams's home in Edward Street. It also occurred to them that credit for Nowak's progress was due to Elsie and her method of instruction rather than to the good old schoolmaster. But they said nothing, for they did not want to hurt the feelings of the dear old man, and army life had taught them a diplomatic reticence of opinion. Mindful of the Captain's threat, they went bravely on : " I want to be a soldier. I want to be a sailor. I want to be a teacher. I want . . ."

Chapter 11

THE BEAUTY OF THE I.C. ENGINE

THE trumpet sounds early every morning and the company marches off for exercises.

The long siestas in the tents are over. Even those who most intensely dislike getting up early were quite fed up with them.

"At least we are doing something" was a slogan of consolation. It reminded one of France. Last year the neighbourhood of the great camp of Coetquidan in Brittany was the scene of similar rehearsals of war. Four Polish divisions and two brigades were organised there and put up a good show when the curtain went up in May.

Every morning a task used to be set :

"Our platoon, acting as advance guard of a larger unit, will go in the direction of Guerney, in security formation. . . ."

"Our company, supported by heavy machine-gun fire, will carry out an attack on La Touche hill. . . ."

"We have to guard the windmills of St. Gurval. . . ."

"Patrols to be sent to the Forest of Comblessac. . . ."

In the course of several months of intensive training, every acre in the district was thoroughly patrolled, taken and retaken in multiple offensives. Even the most poetically minded youths, walking out on a Sunday with their French sweethearts, would make—in moments between the more violent outbursts of passion—remarks like "Tell me, darling, where would you place sentries in this forest ? "

The French girl usually took the question for a trap and racked her brains for its concealed and no doubt highly depraved meaning. But the Pole asked in earnest :

"If the Germans were advancing this way, from

Le Beugnon, where would you place your outposts ? "
" The Germans ?   From Le Beugnon ?   *Pas possible.*
I would run home quickly. . . ."

" You don't understand war at all."   The soldier was
annoyed.   And the Germans did come from Le Beugnon.

Now all this goes on in Scotland.   Only one has not got
to start at 3 a.m. to get to the rifle range, because it's only
eight miles away.   And mock battles are not fought out
on the fields adjoining the village.

In the morning the troops climb on lorries specially
built for that purpose.   There was nothing of that kind in
France.   They drive through Scottish villages which have
not yet had time to start their daily work, and through
green country wet with morning dew, along smooth roads
without any signposts—to an unknown destination.

The mountains and glens of Scotland are an ideal ground
for military manoeuvres.   Some forest for a screen, some
pastures for attack, and a road-crossing which a little
imagination can easily endow with a tremendous strategic
importance.   Farther on, a few lonely houses, a line of
hills and a high mountain like a loaf of bread.   Plenty of
empty open space and of heather.   A paradise for sportsmen
and soldiers.   Motor transport extended the scope of
operations to an extent undreamt of in the days of route
marches.   It's fun to start on a fine morning on a motor
trip into the unknown—a kind of " mystery tour " of the
charabancs.   The tactical task is announced on the spot.

The local farmers are rather puzzled.   " What can
there be about this potato field," asks a farmer, contemporary of the Great Queen ; " they were here twice
last week and here they come again."

*
* *

The platoon, or the company, as the case may be,
advances warily with the whole regulation monkey show
of crawling and jumping.   They are to take a position on
the hill, stubbornly defended by machine guns.   The
attackers keep up a steady fire, too, and climb in leaps and

bounds. The shooting, which is done with blanks, makes a terrific noise. The birds fly in alarm towards the sea, where they are safe ; for no one would dare to fire a shot on the coast for fear of raising an alarm, as though Goering himself had landed on the beach in bathing shorts.

After several hours of running, dropping flat and jumping up again, shooting and shouting, everybody reassembles. Ammunition is carefully put away, commanders check their men and then the whole operation is discussed. The commanding officer speaks about it more earnestly than Allenby would about the taking of Jerusalem or Joffre about the Battle of the Marne. The subordinate officers listen to his opinion as they would to a court martial verdict, and those fortunate enough to earn modest praise feel as though they had just been proposed for a V.C.

Then, muddy from crawling on their bellies, with their shirts soaked to the skin and their tongues hanging out, they return to the lorries. The sight of them is promise of a welcome meal. It does one good to be driven along a fine road after many hours of strenuous exercise. Passing through villages the men sing the old Polish military songs. They wink at the girls with a triumphant air hardly to be surpassed by victors returning from Berlin.

* *

Early in the winter, a new kind of training companion appeared in the field—the tank.

Tanks had been a kind of mythical beast for the Polish soldiers. Poland was too poor to have many. She had neither the resources of Russia, nor the immense industry of Germany, increased by the conquest of Austria and Czechoslovakia. After the last war the Western Democracies subsidised Germany with huge sums, while Poland was completely starved of credits. In consequence the Germans could afford to build thousands of tanks for the next war, while the Poles could not.

But the tanks remained legendary creatures even in France. There were few of them and they were not used much in training. Once in Coetquidan a mock infantry attack against mock trenches was supported by a few mock tanks, gouty veterans of 1917. It was a good show. Creaking and panting, the heavy monsters crept over some barbed wire, splashing the soldiers with mud all over.

A few months later they saw tanks again. This time there were hundreds of them and they were brand new. They moved a good deal faster, but in the wrong direction, for they were German ones.

After the fairly brief experience of May and June the soldiers had better reasons than ever for looking upon tanks as apocalyptic monsters, which appear only in actual warfare, but never on manoeuvres, and crush anyone coming within range. Some formations were to get tanks, but never got them. Some people called themselves an armoured unit ; but they hadn't any tanks either. It was just the same thing all over again.

Suddenly the tanks arrived. Every unit got a few of them. It was also announced that the number was going to be doubled in a few weeks. The announcement met with a sceptical reception.

" We've heard the same story in Coetquidan," said the old hands. When the promised tanks actually were delivered on time, almost on the hour, the men were far more staggered than they would have been by the sudden appearance of twice the number of German tanks. They were used to seeing them and knew more or less how to deal with them, but the appearance of a tank of one's own was something extraordinary and unheard of. War holds in store the most fantastic surprises.

Men looked at the big machines, hardly believing their eyes. The British engineers, pleasant lads, instructed the Polish mechanics and drivers in the use of the new weapons, telling them all about the engines, the caterpillar tracks, the turrets and the rest. They soon got the hang of it and started training. They were not unfamiliar with the theoretical side of the business, but had little practice.

" Well, we'll leave them with you," said the British instructors, returning to the factory. " Take good care of them and be sure to use them soon."

" Oh, yes," said the Poles.

The tanks were henceforth used for training. Previously, the leader of the exercise used to announce : " A column of tanks is attacking you from this forest "—though no tanks were to be seen.

The attacked party then asked : " What type of tanks are they ? " " What is their speed ? How many are there ? " before deciding on the method of defence.

Now the tanks are no longer a product of the imagination. They actually do come out of a forest, climb a slope or attack. They are almost as familiar as the machine guns.

" Now it's different," admitted even the most confirmed grumblers, going to the training ground in lorries.

" Now it's different," thought the soldiers when the tanks, like friendly giants, went ahead in an attack, rattling and roaring, with lumps of earth flying from under their caterpillars.

The tank drivers paraded through Scottish towns with the pride of Roman charioteers returning from a victorious battle. The Polish Army had to come to Britain to make motor transport and tanks an integral part of its equipment.

Chapter 12

SCOTSMEN IN POLAND

"THIS time we won't talk about Scottish and Polish drinks, or about the sentiments which our boys seem to inspire, for unknown reasons, in the female section of the population of this country," said the General on the following evening. "It's time to get down to work—as the commander of my old regiment used to say whenever he saw an unusually large assortment of bottles in the mess. I asked our learned Cadet to prepare a short lecture about Polish-Scottish relations in the course of history. I asked him for it yesterday and to-day he is ready. Good work. Those young chaps, gentlemen, will soon leave us behind unless we are very careful. . . ."

"H'm," grunted the Major. "If it's something like the story about the fellow who resigned his promotion to archbishop because there was no beer, I don't mind history."

"Well, gentlemen," started the graduate of two universities, "you may find it difficult to believe, but there was a time when there were as many Scotsmen in Poland as there are now Poles in Scotland."

"Impossible . . ." muttered the Major.

"To-night we shall also fine you half a crown for every interruption," said the General; "and habitual offenders will pay double."

"Yet it is the truth," continued the Cadet. "It was in the early part of the seventeenth century, when our unhappy country was at the height of its prosperity. France had barely finished her wars of religion. In Germany the North and the South, the Protestants and the Catholics, were conscientiously spending thirty years on murdering and robbing each other. In Spain and in Italy heretics were burnt daily. In Poland alone there were, next to Catholic churches, temples of the Calvinists, Lutherans, Arians, Socinians and Bohemian Brethren, to say nothing of orthodox churches and—an almost unbelievable fact in those times—Moslem mosques. Religion was free, although Poland was a predominantly Catholic country. 'Give us freedom of thought!' Spain appealed in vain to Philip II. In Poland, King Sigismund Augustus said in Parliament: 'I am not king over your consciences.'"

"I would like to tell that to people who think that Poland is a nation with totalitarian traditions," said the General.

"After the Swedish invasion of 1655 there was a little less tolerance. Both Stockholm and Moscow attempted to use for their own purposes the existence of non-Catholic religions in Poland, much as Spain and France had tried to exploit in their interests the presence of Catholics in England. But, before those invasions, Poland was a large and wealthy country, visited by many foreigners, including numerous Scotsmen. Royal charters from the middle of the sixteenth century regulated the position of Scots resident in Poland. William Lithgow, who travelled in Poland in 1616, estimated the number of Scots in that country at 30,000. Sir James Cochrane, Ambassador at the Court of Warsaw in 1652, mentioned the same figure."

"It's about as many as we are here."

"More or less. At any rate, the number was so large that when a plan for a union of England and Scotland under one king was discussed by the English Parliament, in 1606, some English M.P.s opposed it on the ground that England would soon be swamped by Scots, and quoted Poland as an example. One of them painted a gloomy picture. 'If we admit the Scots to our country, they will invade us like cattle breaking through a weak fence from a poor pasture into a rich one, or will spread like a tree transplanted from barren to fertile soil. The crowds of Scotsmen in Poland prove it.' "

" Well, well ! "

" You may well wonder how so many Scotsmen came to be in Poland all at the same time. There were many reasons for their presence there. Some of them were Catholics, who did not very much enjoy life in their native country in the company of Knox. Others were professional soldiers seeking employment where it was to be found. Finally, there were many merchants and traders. The saying, ' Full as a Scotch pedlar's bag,' was current in the Poland of the seventeenth century, for they sold all kinds of wares, such as scarves, thread, needles, knives, mirrors and various other trifles."

" And what about the soldiers ? "

" The Scots have always been a warrior race and they had in Poland plenty of opportunities for proving their valour. The names of many Scottish soldiers of fortune are now forgotten, but some of them achieved prominence or found their way into history by mere chance. For instance, Colonel Alexander Ruthven might be entirely unheard of to-day if it was not for the fact that his widow addressed, in 1605, a petition to the City of Danzig, claiming a pension on the ground that her husband was killed in the service of Sigismund III, King of Poland. She mentioned the fact that Colonel Ruthven was promised before his death, by Chancellor Jan Zamoyski, that his wife and children would not be left unprovided for.

" Among other Scots in Polish service I came across the names of Robert Cunningham (1618) ; Peter Learmonth (1619), who took part in the war against Russia ; Roman Fergusson ; James Wilson and Captain Kirkpatrick (1621). They all received royal commissions or grants, and I have seen the old parchments in Cracow archives before this war. During the invasion of Poland by Carolus Gustavus of Sweden (1655–1656), the famous General Patrick Gordon of Auchleuchries served the King of Poland.

In 1660 he distinguished himself in the victorious battle
of Cudnow, fought by the Poles against the Russians, or,
to be more accurate, the Muscovites.

" In 1671 another Scot, George Bennet, was King John
Casimir's private secretary. In 1673 the following Scottish
gentlemen received from the King and Parliament admission
to the ranks of Polish nobility, with all the privileges
which it carried : Chalmers, Forsyth, Fraser, Gordon,
Halyburton, Watson, Kaskettle, Lindesay, Macfarlant,
Mackay, Miller, Murison, Ogilvie, Patterson and Bonar.
Strange names, perhaps, for Polish noblemen. But they
were well known to the Polish gentry, who accepted them
as ' brothers,' which was the form of address used between
the citizens of the Royal Republic.

" In the ' Trilogy ' of Sienkiewicz, that great epic of
seventeenth-century Poland, the gallant officer who, together
with Wolodyjowski, blew up the fortress of Kamieniec
Podolski rather than abandon it to the Turks, was Kettling,
a Scotsman.

" That's right," cried the Major ; " what a memory
you have ! "

" Your memory, dear Major," said the General, " is not
quite so good, for you've forgotten about the half-crown
fine, although it was arranged at a rather more recent date
than the capture of Kamieniec."

" About fifty years later," continued the speaker,
" Europe was thrilled by a ·rather extraordinary Polish-
Scottish marriage. The Young Pretender, Prince Charles
Edward, known as Bonnie Prince Charlie, married the
granddaughter of Jan Sobieski, King of Poland. It was
an extremely romantic affair, for Princess Clementine was
a guest of her uncle, the Austrian Emperor, and lived in
one of the Hapsburg castles, in which the young Stuart
was not in great favour."

" The wicked Hapsburg hardly guessed that his
descendants would also be mere pretenders . . ."

" The Colonel will pay half a crown for his political

acumen," observed the General, pleased to have caught the Colonel at last.

"Prince Charles Edward's trusted friends spirited the young lady skilfully from the castle, and when her guardians realised what had happened, it was too late. The grand-daughter of the finest leader of Polish cavalry could ride well, for she crossed the Tyrol on horseback and rode through the Brenner to Rome, where she married her Scottish lover. It was a regular scandal and a source of much gossip at all the Courts of Europe. Some disapproved and some sympathised with the romantic couple. . . ."

"What was the outcome of this first Polish-Scottish marriage?" asked the Colonel. "Surely it is important to-day to know how they turn out."

"Indeed it is," the General agreed. "There will be no fine this time, for this is a relevant question." •

"Unfortunately, not all romances end well. Perhaps poor Princess Clementine was not as handsome as her husband, and after some time he turned his attentions elsewhere. The activities of another Scotsman made the matrimonial situation even worse. The Princess's dowry had been invested in various securities, including those floated by the famous financier Law, the Dr. Schacht of those times, who did not worry about gold cover for his bonds. Eventually he crashed and large numbers of people were ruined."

"But what happened to Charles and Clementine?"

"The disappointed wife left her husband and found religious consolation in one of the convents of Rome. It is said that Bonnie Prince Charlie, who loved his wife and had sought among beautiful Italian women merely compensation for his political failures, desired a reconciliation. But Clementine died young, before he could achieve it. Such was the end of the marriage which united for a moment two countries and two noble houses. There was no heir to the names of Stuart and of Sobieski."

"*Sic transit gloria mundi*," observed the Chaplain.

"The further course of Polish-Scottish relations," went on the Cadet, "was somewhat less exciting. After the Polish insurrection of 1830–31, which was suppressed by the Tsar, Thomas Campbell founded the 'Literary Society of Friends of Poland,' which did much to assist the Polish political exiles in England and Scotland between 1830 and 1863, the date of another rising. After the failure of the second national insurrection, the Society redoubled its efforts and carried on its work almost to the end of the century. Many Poles found hospitality in Scotland. The great Captain George Gilfillow writes in his memoirs about the sermons and speeches which he had made in many towns of Scotland on behalf of Poland. After 1863, interest in Poland subsided in England, but in Scotland the famous poem ending with the words 'And Freedom shrieked when Kosciuszko fell' was still to be found in all the school textbooks. Every Scottish child learned to look upon Poland as a bastion of freedom. No wonder that the Polish Army is to-day hospitably received in Scotland."

"It's very interesting," said the General ; "who could have expected such close relations ? It's a long way from Scotland to Poland, and yet they have a lot in common. The English book which you were quoting must be very interesting. What a pity I can't read English ! "

"It is a bilingual pamphlet," said the Cadet, "published in English and Polish by the British Ministry of Information."

"Really ? How did you get hold of it ? "

"It was here, in this library, even before we came here, sir."

"So it was ; of course it was here," the General admitted. "I noticed it, but did not read it. Oh, yes, army life, especially at the front, does cut you off from those intellectual pleasures which we are all missing so much. Hard times, these."

"One can sometimes find interesting things even in books," observed the Major, with conviction.

Chapter 13

CHURCHILL

THEY had been up before dawn. That is easily accomplished in a Scottish November of long nights, encroaching on the day at both ends.

The billets are inspected for the fourth time.

" Are the boots polished ? "

They have been polished incessantly since the previous night and acquired a chromium-plated finish, on which the men try to improve by using cunning methods of shoeblack rubbed on a moist foundation. Even the Sergeant-Major, who served in Poland in the President's guard of honour at Warsaw Castle, and knew all about polishing shoes and buttons, was satisfied at last.

" Well, well," he said to the young soldiers who stormed Narvik. " I may be able yet to teach you something about real soldiering."

The rifles, cleaned for hours, are free from the smallest speck of dust, to say nothing of rust. Belts ? Helmets ? Gas masks ? Everything in perfect order. Nothing was found wanting on that day in any of the huts.

The Company Commander, not an easy man to please, was puzzled. " What is the matter with them to-day ? Is it the review ? Or maybe the weather ? "

It was a dismal rainy day and the heavy clouds coming from the sea seemed to be merely big lumps of spray churned up by the waves.

" Tell me, Sergeant, have you ever seen anything like it in Poland ? Rheumatism is about all we will bring back. And the bloody review. . . . What is it this time ? "

" It's that . . . you know, Shurshill."

The Sergeant, who had served in many wars, did not get on with English any better than he had done before with French, German, Italian, Serbian, Rumanian or Hungarian, or in fact any other language. Only Russian, known for the fantastic riches of its swearing repertory, held for him a certain attraction. In August he had looked on with some disgust when young boys stared eagerly at difficult English words written on a blackboard put up in a field. Not that he had any objection to English spelling in particular, but he never did think much of the art of writing or reading in any language, including Polish. He often marvelled why so many monuments were erected in honour of the inventor of printing, while the merit of the inventor of goose-stepping went practically unrecognised.

"What's the use of turning a decent army into a damned university, with foreign languages, too," he muttered. "They waste time instead of learning something useful, like salute in march . . . or reporting to an officer. . . ."

"Ah ! it's Shurshill," the Captain said. "It's Shurshill himself."

"Well, it's Shurshill," said the Sergeant, meekly ; "if it has to be."

The Captain smiled. He knew the old Sergeant's soul through and through. Ever since Churchill's visit to Polish camps in Scotland had been announced, the subject was discussed. The Sergeant once asked the Captain :

"Who is he, sir ? A General ? "

"No. He is Prime Minister."

"Prime Minister, and he not a General ? "

The Captain chuckled. "Yes. He is Prime Minister, though not a General."

"A civilian ? "

For the old professional N.C.O. the Commander-in-Chief is God Almighty. The Generals—his saints. The barracks—the best place in an otherwise unsatisfactory world, and the saluting of officers the basis of civilisation.

" A civilian ?   Oh, Lord, a civilian. . . ."

The Sergeant said nothing ; he was too well disciplined
for that. But it was a deep shock. He could understand
a visit of the President of Poland, a tall white-haired
gentleman, slim and fine-looking. He could understand
very well special parades for the Commander-in-Chief,
General Sikorski. He understood perfectly well the visit
of Lord Gort (a General and a Lord, too : that's something);
or of the other . . . what's his name? . . . Sir . . . English
names were a more impenetrable barrier to the old fellow
than the thickest barbed wire. He thoroughly approved
the visit of H.R.H. the Duke of Kent. In his military
heart, faithful though he was to the Republic, there was a
very special feeling for a King and everything connected
with the throne. The young and handsome Duke, in his
R.A.F. uniform, made a good impression on the Sergeant.

But now it was going to be Churchill.

His confusion was increased by the fact that the company
of which he was one of the pillars was composed largely
of young fellows, many of them university graduates.
The Sergeant would have exchanged them gladly any day
for a bunch of country yokels from Eastern Poland, where
the rule of the Tsars left a tradition of servility and the
peasantry were tough and easily pleased. They made
good soldiers. He knew that his company of lawyers and
engineers knew more than it was good for any man to know,
and he never was quite certain what reactions to expect
from them. Take, for instance, that Churchill visit. The
Sergeant had become resigned long ago to the fact that
this so-called army was sinfully indifferent to the beauty
and the profound meaning of military parades. He had
heard in the huts, before every official visit, comments which
only the greatest indulgence could excuse on the ground
of tender age. That is why the excitement and eagerness
before Churchill's visit seemed to him almost suspicious.

" You never know with those university gentlemen,"

he complained to the storekeeper, a man of similar views ;
" what's poison to them on Tuesday becomes meat on
Thursday. First they hate it and then they ask for it
themselves. Make sense of them if you can."

He hesitated and added : " Do you know what they like
so much about that Shurshill ? "

The storekeeper did not know. This was hardly
surprising, for he never left the storeroom and he knew
of all the countries which he had visited—and they were
many—only the inside of their military equipment stores.
The Sergeant decided to find out about Churchill by
skilfully questioning his own subordinates, without, of
course, shattering their assumed respect for a superior's
omniscience. His casual questions did not reveal very
much. He learned that Churchill was the descendant of
some Duke called Marlborough, which sounded all right,
but considerably complicated the whole matter. He also
gathered that he had been an antagonist of Chamberlain,
but then he knew even less about Chamberlain than he did
about Churchill, so that did not help much. He heard
that his mother was American, and this was to him the
unmistakable symbol of wealth ; America being inhabited
mostly by millionaires. But it was all rather mysterious.
Then someone made a remark which completely staggered
the Sergeant. What did Churchill do before the war ?
Oh, he wrote articles, books. . . .

Wrote books and articles ! If it was books alone—but
articles ! The writing of articles was considered by the
Sergeant to be a flippant occupation, to say the very least.
Journalism was for him something closely akin to fire-
swallowing practised at country fairs, circus-clowning or
gipsy fortune-telling. Strange antecedents, indeed, for a
British Prime Minister. They even said that he was very
well, paid for his articles. The Sergeant pondered on the
incalculable ways of this world.

He abandoned all further investigation on the subject
of the mystery man.

" He may be this or that," he concluded, " but the review will be first-rate. As usual."

**

The review promised to be better than usual. The Sergeant noticed little things, invisible to the layman—the way soldiers went out of the barracks, formed fours and rehearsed for the last time some movements. Then they marched to the other end of the town and waited in the rain. They had for company some sheep and envied their patience and detachment, natural in wearers of white woolly wigs.

Some cars passed by on a road washed clean by days of rain. " Attention ! " The sharp command pulled them up and sent a thrill through their bones. Other orders followed and set the troops in motion, as a throbbing starter sets going a powerful engine.

" Company ! March ! "

One battalion after another, they marched with a steady step, tensely expectant. The eyes of the commanders followed them closely, for they were anxious to avoid the slightest gap in the ranks ; the slightest irregularity. Their men were to be judged on their appearance and marching discipline. A forest of rifles moved along the Scottish road. It was so dense that the soldiers could see little ahead.

Then a new order, for those already on the march : " Company ! March ! "

The forest of rifles grew higher. The step of the column became harder, stiffer. The right hand, outstretched, moved rhythmically up and down. Up to the waist and then down again. Up and down. A thunder of hundreds of feet on the macadam.

A band beside the road struck up a march, but the lively tune seemed damped by the moist air and the bleak sky, hanging low and heavy over the rain-soaked landscape. There was another command : " Eyes right ! "

Section after section, on coming to the spot, threw their

heads sharply to the right. All eyes turned right. All faces were grim and all chins stuck out.

" So that's him," thought the Sergeant.

" Churchill ! Churchill ! " thought the soldiers.

Next to General Sikorski there was a man in a grey Burberry, streaming with water. Heavy and broad, with a large, powerful face. He seemed to be deliberate in movement, but strangely alert. He stood and watched.

The soldiers looked towards him not only in obedience to the words of the command. There was curiosity in their stare and something more—hope. And there was a desperate desire to show this stern and strong man what they are. To show him their own strength.

The rain flogged the soldiers' helmets, the Scottish fields, Sikorski's square-topped cap and Churchill's bare head. He was saluting with the civilian salute, hat in hand. Whom ? The colours, which had passed long ago ? The commanders, standing a few steps behind him ? Or perhaps those who had crossed many frontiers at the risk of their lives—the soldiers ? Nobody knew what he was thinking about, watching Polish troops marching along a Scottish road on a melancholy November day.

*
* *

" Thank you, General," he said to Sikorski. " They are good soldiers. All they want is equipment."

" Yes, equipment . . ."

" They will have it," said Winston Churchill.

The men were vanishing in the mist and the steady rhythm of their feet was still heard when they went out of sight, marching on.

*
* *

" That Churchill," said the Sergeant in a rare moment of effusion, after returning to the billets ; " that's a man. He just has to look at a man—tough."

And in spite of the rain and cold, in spite of the exhausting march, there was a warmer and a happier feeling than usual on that day in the soldiers' huts.

The whole afternoon, with a good picture at the local cinema and a lot of dates fixed a long time ago, went west. But this time no one minded.

Chapter 14

THROUGH SCOTTISH EYES

"WELL, gentlemen," said the General, who hated cards, but liked long fireside talks, "has it occurred to any of you to think what we look like to our dear hosts in this country?"

The members of the staff said nothing. Everyone was answering the question for himself, and finally the Colonel ventured to voice his conclusion : "My opinion is they think well of us. They see in us victims of misfortune and faithful allies; they know that the Poles fought in the far north and are fighting in Libya; they have heard about the part played by our airmen in the Battle of Britain . . ."

" I am afraid they have good reason to think the worst," said the Major, usually a dissenter. " We are filling their towns with noise and babel. Our soldiers are in the habit of singing, or rather howling, at the top of their voices. We are, by comparison with them, both rowdy and gloomy, we are . . ."

" Here are the views of a sceptic and an enthusiast," observed the General. " Of course, there are some of each type among those who see us, but what do you think is the opinion of an average person, neither sour nor sentimental ? What do you think about it?" He turned to the Cadet.

" It's hard to say, sir."

" What is hard ? At your age, I used to. . . . And you know English. You were in this country before we came and you must have seen many places and noticed the opinion about Poles."

" But it is difficult to sum it up in a word."

" Who asked you to say it in a word?" protested the

General. " On the contrary. There is plenty of time ; it's raining so hard that nobody will think of going out and it's Sunday afternoon. There is nothing better at such a time than a good instructive talk. Please stay with us, Major." He waved back the fugitive, who was trying to sneak away quietly. " We should be sad without you. I meant this little lecture specially for you. I feel sure you will be interested. And there will be no fine for interruptions."

The Major sighed and sank back in his chair.

" I could hardly reply to your question by a direct statement," said the Cadet. " It is a fact that to them we are quite different and sometimes mysterious people. I hope to make it clearer in the little story which I am going to tell to-day."

" I see that it will be another Sunday well spent," concluded the General. " Let's get down to the job, gentlemen. Who wants whisky and who wants sherry ? Let's start."

The Cadet began his story amidst a pleasant noise of popping corks and tinkling glasses.

Cadet Walewski's story about the Provost of Invermuchty, who turned his burgh into a fortress

The Provost of Invermuchty (the real name of which cannot be disclosed for reasons of National Defence) was seriously perturbed. In spite of a glorious past, to which the ruins of the castle testified, the ruins of the abbey and the ruins of an inn frequented by the Pretender ; in spite of numerous attractions—the town of Invermuchty was still without its Polish garrison six months after the Poles invaded the country.

" I know the symptoms," said the Major. " When we were in Brittany, in the winter of 1939, the mayors of the neighbouring towns used to fight for a garrison. After all, the men leave all their pay in the local pubs."

" Excuse me," said the Cadet, " but it was not quite the

same thing in this case. This is not France, where the
bourgeois virtue of money-grabbing replaced the knightly
traditions of more elegant robbery ; this is Scotland, where
tradition and the past count for a lot, whether for a man or
for a town. . . ."

" Go on," said the General.

" The Provost of Invermuchty began to fear that the
war might soon be over and his burgh might miss an
opportunity that comes once in a thousand years. He
realised that in these islands one does not often get a
chance of having a foreign garrison, let alone one so exotic.
He was annoyed at the thought that miserable settlements
founded only two or three hundred years ago would be
able to mention in their chronicles such an interesting visit,
and his city, founded under Malcolm IV, would have
nothing to write down against the year 1940. The city
charter was given by Mary Stuart, and James VI released
the burghers from the obligation of entertaining him ;
while Bonnie Prince Charlie stayed four days. Afterwards
the town was rewarded for this ill-timed hospitality by the
gift of a garrison of Hanoverians."

" The Provost of Invermuchty was too proud to solicit
distinction. None of his honourable predecessors
would have stooped to such an action. He knew what
was his due, by seniority and tradition, but he said
nothing."

" Eventually, however, the news came through that
Invermuchty would be garrisoned and defended by a
Polish formation."

" Oh ! we'll be speaking Polish, too," cried the school-
children. " I am sure you will show those Catholics from
the Continent how a Puritan girl behaves," said the
Minister.

" There will be boys to go with to the pictures, to tea
and to the pastry shop," thought the Puritan girls.

" We have had in our time Normans and Englishmen,
Hanoverians and Irishmen ; now we are going to have

Poles as well," thought the Provost with modest satisfaction.

**

First the motor cycles, then the quartermasters, and finally the troops. There was about one company, with a few auxiliary nucleus formations, with an anti-tank gun, liaison services, mortars and machine guns. There was also a staff, and everything was commanded by a Polish Colonel with a rainbow of ribbons on his left breast. He was a stern, gaunt man with a haggard face tanned brown by the wind and made fiercer by a pair of menacing eyebrows. He walked as though he were a heavy tank. ("A good portrait in the Town Hall would be a fine legacy to future generations," thought the Provost.)

He greeted the Colonel with a splendid speech in which he referred to every one of the glorious events which made the history of the city what it was. Even the stag hunt of Robert Bruce was mentioned and particularly stressed, as likely to appeal to inhabitants of Russian forests full of wild beasts.

The Colonel was pleased with the speech, to which he listened as though he had understood it. Then he replied with another magnificent speech, mostly on the subject of a certain Polish regiment, which was to be rebuilt around his unit. One gathered that it was the regiment responsible for the rout of Genghis Khan, who would have certainly gone as far as Scotland if he had not been stopped in time. Later on, the same regiment defeated the Germans in East Prussia, at a place called Grunwald ; then after another interval of a few centuries it smashed the power of the Turk at Vienna and continued the good work by beating the Spaniards at Somosierra, the Bolsheviks at Warsaw, and finally coming to Invermuchty to prepare for new victories.

The Provost listened to the Colonel's long speech with keen interest, slightly alarmed by the large number of consonants, but reassured by the rolling 'rr's. He believed

that the Colonel had expounded his prophecies concerning
the progress of the war and praised Scotland. At the
luncheon which followed, the mutual understanding was
finally cemented. The Provost appreciated the Colonel's
interest in history and his opinion was reciprocated. It was
decided that on the following day they would go together
for a long walk, to see the immediate environs of the town ;
the village on the other side of the river and some
neighbouring hills.

"He is probably a lover of nature," thought the Provost
with satisfaction, and decided that he rather liked the Poles.

* *
*

On the following day, at 10 a.m., the Provost, the Colonel
and two officers, accompanied by an interpreter, set out
on their expedition, respectfully greeted by the citizens
as they drove through the streets. The camouflaged
military car took them on to the Perth road. After a few
hundred yards the Colonel stopped the car and the whole
party got out. The Colonel unfolded a large staff map.

"He has to find his bearings," explained the interpreter.
The Provost tried to suggest that as he knew every inch
of the countryside, where he had played Robinson Crusoe
and Indians as a boy, the use by the Colonel of a map with
strange names was rather superfluous.

When the Provost's remark was translated, the Colonel
shook his head and politely but firmly refused.

"The Colonel says," the interpreter tried to mediate,
"that the Polish Army regulations forbid officers to use
the assistance of the inhabitants, requesting them to rely
only on their maps."

The Provost wanted to say : "After all, we are Allies
and this is our country," but he said nothing.

The Colonel looked at the map, then at the country,
then again at the map and he said a few words, which the
interpreter eagerly transmitted to the Provost : "The
Colonel likes this neighbourhood."

"All right," thought the Provost, pacified ; "those

Polish officers appreciate natural beauty. I always thought they were pleasant, civilised and sensitive people. They're just a bit odd. . . ."

His love of Scottish scenery carried the Colonel to the top of a small hill, which was very muddy at that time of the year. Then it took him down into a gully, along which a romantic stream wound its way amidst shrubs and alders. The Provost felt a nasty gurgling of water in his shoes, for it was a place which remained wet for most of the year and was always flooded in the autumn. The boots of the Colonel and his officers, made in Warsaw, the home of some of the finest riding and hunting boots in the world, stood the test well. But the town footwear of the City Father was not meant for this kind of wading. The miserable host, muddy and soaked to the skin, went on, wavering between proud elation at the sight of such enthusiasm for Scottish nature and despair at the prospect of a bad cold. The Colonel made matters worse by staying a particularly long time on the marshy ground by the stream. He walked up and down, looking round with considerable interest.

" Why on earth should the Poles have such a liking for mud ? " marvelled the most patient and long-suffering of Scottish Provosts.

" The Colonel likes this pasture very much," said the interpreter by way of explanation.

" It is rather good," admitted the local patriot ; " but very muddy at the present time."

His remark was faithfully passed on to the Colonel, who did not, however, share his view.

" The Colonel says the mud is splendid. The Colonel says he likes the mud very much. The Colonel inquires how long you have such mud here."

" They are a lot of storks from Poland," thought the Provost. " They like mud. They will ask me next whether the frogs are good." But he summoned his last reserves of courtesy and replied politely : " As for the mud, it dries up only for two weeks in August ; if there is plenty of sunny weather. Sometimes it never dries at all. We have been planning for a long time to have this slope drained. But the cost of labour went up since the Socialists were in Government and farming did not pay."

It occurred to him that such a neglected piece of land, quite near to town, too, might make a bad impression on representatives of an agricultural nation.

" But now it's all changed. In wartime we need all the fodder there is and prices have gone up. Farming is very important nowadays. Next spring we shall certainly drain this place and it will yield a lot of good hay."

The Colonel, when this well-meant promise was interpreted to him, barked a good deal in a language which sounds harsh at any time.

" The Colonel says that this little valley should not be drained until the end of the war. It would be better to flood that field over there."

" But there are those lovely vegetable gardens," groaned the Provost.

The Colonel grinned shortly with evil mirth.

" The Poles love mud and hate vegetables," concluded the harassed Provost of one of the most historic towns of beautiful Scotland, " but they are our Allies and guests. Still, they are very peculiar."

He felt much relieved when his Ally and guest stepped back on to the hard surface of the road.

They went up to an old stone-built mill house of the time of Queen Anne, and the Colonel inspected it with interest. He admired the thickness of the ancient walls. He climbed a ladder to see the attic. He even punched a hole in the rotting wooden roof and pushed his head through to scan the country all round.

" Maybe he was a painter before the war ? Or maybe a landscape photographer ? He is probably looking for the best viewpoint," thought the Provost, and the old

miller was completely dumbfounded at the sight of a hole
in his roof made deliberately by a senior officer, who
seemed otherwise sober.

Then they walked up the hill by the forest; then they
came down on the pasture and later went to the ruins of a
Catholic abbey destroyed by the Puritans of Cromwell.
The Provost was panting, for the officers walked quickly
and talked so much that they hardly noticed him. He felt
rewarded for his hardships by the fact that they were
people who took a keener and more thorough interest in
the country than any of the tourists which had visited it in
thousands. They seemed to be really appreciative. When
they reached the hillside dominating the town, a magnificent
view of Invermuchty opened before them. The Provost,
forgetting the dangers of rheumatism, sat on a boulder and
looked in silent reproach at his Polish companions. They
stood a little higher, and the Colonel, his rough-hewn
countenance fiercer than ever, was explaining something
to his officers in short, forceful sentences. Sometimes he
looked at his map and then pointed a commanding arm at
some point of the landscape, which was indeed beautiful.
The officers sometimes ventured timid remarks. On the
whole, they seemed content to read the thoughts of the
master in his eyes, or follow the thrust of his finger at
some noteworthy object.

"He looks rather like the Iron Duke at Waterloo,"
thought the Provost, "or Kitchener at Khartoum. Britain
has a great navy, but Poland has great soldiers. They
manage to look as though they were commanding huge
armies even when taking a simple country walk."

Eventually the war council finished its debates and the
magnificent Colonel suddenly became aware of the presence
of his civilian British companion, honouring him with his
first smile of the day. The Provost sensed in it the
expression of a strange but very manly friendship.

"Please," said the Colonel and talked for a while to the
interpreter, who immediately cabled the message on.

"The Colonel says that he is quite satisfied with the neighbourhood."

"Satisfied?" thought the Provost. "He probably meant that he likes it." But he gracefully acknowledged the compliment.

"The Colonel thinks that only few improvements will be necessary to fit this bit of country for its task."

"What task? How can scenery have a task? The interpreter probably mixed it up," were the alarmed thoughts which flashed through the Provost's mind.

"Nevertheless, a few alterations will be necessary."

The Provost glanced at the familiar spread of country, which he had known since his childhood. The Colonel's statement reminded him strangely of the words of one of Edinburgh's best dental surgeons, who had told him only two days ago: "There is nothing the matter with your teeth. We shall just have to remove those two at the top, this one at the back and one wisdom tooth, file off these two cutters and fit gold crowns to this one on the left and that one on the right. That will be all."

The Colonel assisted the interpreter with eloquent gestures. "First of all, it will be necessary to put up the level of the stream, by making this dyke higher. . . ."

"But the water would then flood the vegetable gardens on the left bank!" gasped the Provost.

"That is exactly what we want," said the interpreter with quiet sadism; "those gardens and also some of the fields. That is most important."

The Provost was stunned.

"Then," continued the interpreter, explaining the broad sweep of the Colonel's hand, "all those trees by the river will have to be cut down."

"Alder trees"—the soul of the nature-lover was twisting on the rack—"but these old alder trees are one of the principal beauties of the countryside!"

"They form an obstacle," said the interpreter, firmly.

"But there is an open field all around."

" That is exactly what we want—bare open fields everywhere."

The Provost was flabbergasted again. The Colonel's hand, hovering over the hillside like a vulture seeking its prey, pointed to a pasture on which a flock of sheep was peacefully grazing.

" Here there will be a deep ditch."

" But there is a ditch there already," moaned the Provost ; " deep enough to hide a sheep."

The officers shook with satanic laughter when the Provost's reply was interpreted to them. He listened to the words of the interpreter with the feelings of the accused who sees the black cap on the head of the judge.

" There will have to be a real ditch, twelve feet deep and fifteen feet wide. In that bowl there will be an obstacle wall nine feet high. Those debris with ivy all over them . . ."

" They are the ruins of the Catholic Abbey," gasped the Provost.

" . . . will be blown up with dynamite. That copse will be cut down. This farm . . ."

The Colonel interjected a few words.

" No, this farm can stay. It may be useful. So you see that the Colonel was right when he said that the Scottish landscape is satisfactory. Much can be made of it with only minor changes."

Suddenly the Provost understood everything in a blinding flash. He understood why the Polish officers' love of scenery took such a strange form. He understood the walk over marshes which was certain to give him a cold and maybe 'flu. He even realised why he had unconsciously associated it all with a visit to the dentist.

" So you want to turn this place into a battlefield ? "

This intelligent guess met with the Colonel's approval.

" The Colonel says that he is glad to see that you, although a civilian, have grasped so well the purpose of our plan. He is even willing to explain to you the whole plan of 'arming the ground,' as we say, and preparing it for its important task. The flooding of this little valley will make it impassable for German tanks, even of the lighter type. . . ."

The Provost shuddered at the thought that German tanks could not only land in Scotland, but actually come to this pasture, on which sheep were peacefully grazing. But he also felt a flush of excitement at the thought that the apparently insignificant stream near Invermuchty might become the grave of a host of armoured monsters. He listened with interest.

" The heavy machine guns from the mill house, supported by the fire of Bren guns from the forest, will have a very good field of fire, especially after we have cut down those trees."

" My poor alders ! " A wave of pity swept the Provost's heart, followed by a new feeling of resentment. " Why did they grow there ? "

" The anti-tank ditch across this field will form a sufficient obstacle to stop them for a while. The anti-tank guns, placed here, will have a neat little job to do."

" How they enjoy the idea," thought the Provost, and he suddenly visualised to himself smashed tanks in a ditch, a mass of iron and men, lashed by the short-range fire of guns, churning and breaking the swarming chaos of machinery.

" Here," explained the interpreter, " we shall lay the main curtain of machine-gun fire."

" Curtain of fire ? "

" Here, there will be slicing fire. . . ."

The Provost, whose health had kept him in the rear lines during the last war, was duly impressed.

" Our heavy machine guns from behind the road will control all those fields, as far as those houses."

" But you can't see them from the road," objected the Provost.

The officers chuckled. " It will be indirect fire, carrying

over that hillside. It's a matter of reckoning, indirect fire. Splendid thing. We hope you will soon see for yourself. . . ."

German ghosts appeared again on the peaceful fields of Invermuchty.

" Those passages will be kept closed with fire. This gully—a very dangerous spot—will be covered by mortars and bomb throwers. It's a dead field. . . ."

" But there is no field there," observed the Provost ; " just shrubs and junipers. That isn't a field."

" But it's dead. You don't see what we mean by that. We may have to put there anti-tank mines. As to anti-aircraft defence, the church tower seems to have been built specially for that purpose. The roof of the church is quite good, too. The mill is also useful. It's just sufficiently concealed."

All eyes turned towards the romantic ruins of the old abbey, overgrown with ivy.

" What's this useless rubbish ? It produces another dead field."

" It was a Catholic abbey, ravaged in 1653 by Cromwell's ruffians," said the Provost, hoping to appeal to the Popish instincts of the Poles.

" Cromwell was right," said the Colonel ; " and it's a pity he did not finish the job properly. A soldier should be buttoned to the last button and he should wreck to the last stone. We will do what Cromwell left undone."

Then he turned to the Provost with words of comfort : " You see that a few minor alterations will make this place quite decent. Well, let's go home. It's time for lunch."

*
* *

The 'flu which the Provost developed immediately on his return from the country walk in company with Polish officers, turned at night into a fever with hallucinations. His family listened in terror to his wild babbling about German tanks sinking in mud, about barrages on the roof of the mill, dead fields and Cromwell's soldiery. The doctor, who arrived at dawn, found the patient asleep, exhausted with nightmares.

" I don't know what it may mean, doctor, but he talked about fire. He spoke about fire of all sorts—side fire, indirect fire and fire barrages. It all sounded terrible."

" I am afraid, Colonel," the interpreter observed after lunch, " that we shall have a difficult job with this Provost ; he will never consent to the cutting down of the alders, or the flooding of the fields, or the destruction of the ruins."

" He has to, because we have been entrusted with organising the defence of this sector," replied the Colonel, calmly. " Besides, though I may not know English, I know human nature. This man will consent. Do you know why ? Because he has a sense of history."

" That is exactly the reason why he will protest against the destruction of ruins which even Cromwell spared. . . ."

" That is why he will agree. . . ."

The Provost was ill on Tuesday and Wednesday. He talked to no one and struggled with his thoughts. On Thursday he was visited by some of the more prominent councillors. He addressed them with some hesitation.

" Gentlemen, I have important information to share with you. As in the past, our city is faced with certain necessities of war. I may describe them as historical necessities."

" The immediate neighbourhood of Invermuchty has been included in one of the internal defence lines."

" The Polish Commander, who has just arrived, inspected the ground together with me."

" In his opinion it is eminently suitable for defence action and the stopping of even the most serious armoured raids."

" But, in the view of this distinguished military expert, some . . . h'm, improvements may be necessary. . . ."

At this moment the speaker took a deep breath, as though he was about to dive.

" It will be unfortunately necessary to fell our alder

trees by the stream, for they seem to be obstructing the . . . field of fire. It will be necessary to put up the locks, so as to flood not only the marshy ground which was to be drained, but also some of the gardens up stream . . . you know which place I mean."

" Yes, we know," the councillors nodded without particular enthusiasm.

" A deep ditch will have to be dug across the pasture on the hillside. It will have to be so wide that really almost half the pasture will be gone. . . .

" We will also have to cut down some trees on the edge of the wood.

" And, finally, my friends, I must tell you that what still remains of the ruins of the old abbey will have to be blown up with dynamite, because it obstructs the enemy's most likely line of approach." The unfortunate speaker breathed a deep sigh of relief, as after making a most horrible confession. As the room remained silent, he added, mournfully : " Also old Cliff's mill and the church, especially the belfry and the roof, will be used for purposes of anti-aircraft defence. I think that will be all."

The silence which met his speech frightened the Provost. Nobody said a word. Nobody even moved. They seemed not to have understood, and he dreaded a new explanation. " They probably think I gave way to foreigners." At last, unable to bear it any longer, the Provost said : " Well, what do you think about it ? "

The butcher, McCullen, dour and critical, taciturn and suspicious, muttered : " Anyway, those Poles don't take the King's Money for nothing."

It was a cryptic remark and the Provost did not feel reassured at all.

" What do you mean by that ? " he asked uneasily.

" I think," said the butcher, " that they don't sit twiddling their thumbs, but get right down to the job. They've hardly arrived and they are already digging trenches, putting up obstacles and finding gun emplacements.

They seem to mean to defend us in earnest. They started work on the road yesterday. Hard workers."

"Well, yes," replied the Provost, feeling slightly happier ; "but they want to give us more marshes, cut down trees and destroy ancient monuments. . . ."

McCullen shrugged his heavy shoulders. "I always thought you set too much store by such things. You like it dry here and wet there, with a few nice trees and ruins to order. What's the use of it ? What will be the good of your vegetable garden after the German tanks have passed here ? What's the use of the willows by the river—except to boys and their lassies in the summer ? "

"That's right," said another councillor, who had two young daughters and was rather worried by their walks by the river.

"Or take the ruins of the abbey," went on the savage butcher. "What's the use of them ? They're neither pretty nor interesting. Just a heap of old rubbish."

"Quite right," nodded the grocer, whose son had studied history of art in Edinburgh.

"Anyone can see that Cromwell wrecked all that there was useful about it and the rest was left in the rain for three hundred years until what remained is little more good than your teeth, if you don't mind my saying so."

"I don't care for your personal choice of comparisons."

"I am very sorry. It just occurred to me, without meaning to hurt you."

"I suggest that we help them to carry out the work as quickly as possible. I suppose you asked us to come to discuss the best way of doing it ? "

"Yes, h'm, of course, that is what I wanted to do. . . ."

"Well, then, let's get on with it."

"But, gentlemen," the Provost tried to temporise, "don't you feel that scenery known and loved since childhood . . . that relics of our town's glorious past . . . that all that is dearest to us and that stands for our tradition . . . ? "

A fourth councillor, who had not spoken so far, addressed the Provost persuasively : " My dear friend, we all understand your sorrow, which everyone of us is sharing. But just think. The alder trees are lovely and many of us used to take our girls for a walk along the river when we were young. There are good vegetables in the gardens up there and excellent hay where they want to dig that huge ditch. And the ruins, though they no longer have any style, look nice in the autumn when the ivy gets brownish and gleams a rich colour. But just think of this : What will happen if we keep it all and then history says ' the German invasion force broke through our defence line near Invermuchty, which was insufficiently fortified owing to the opposition of its Provost, Mr. . . .' ? "

" Exactly," hissed the butcher, in a menacing tone.

" My opposition ? " wailed the Provost in renewed torment.

"Whose else ? And now think of this : What if historians write that ' the German invasion was finally defeated on the defence lines of Invermuchty, thanks to the public spirit of its citizens, who flooded the low fields, dug deep ditches, cut down trees and destroyed the ruins of an old abbey, thus turning the whole region into a powerful fortified line. The fields of Invermuchty were strewn with hundreds of smashed tanks and thousands of German corpses. . . .' ? "

The Provost's historical imagination, accustomed to looking into the past, took for the first time in his life a peep into the future.

" What a lot of tourists will come to Invermuchty to see the battlefield. And what tourists ? Americans. Just like the French battlefields, only better." The prospect thrilled the Provost's brother-in-law, the local hotel owner and a canny business man.

His utilitarian view met with general contempt. Everyone was pondering the glorious vision of fame brought to Invermuchty.

" St. Andrews and Edinburgh and all the castles will be
just nothing to it," observed even the matter-of-fact butcher.

" Of course," said the Provost, " they will be simply
nowhere."   And, moved by a sudden resolution, he left
his bed.

" I am sorry, gentlemen," he said, " but I believe that
the honour of our city demands that I should inform our
Allies as early as possible of Invermuchty's decision to
help them in whatever way they may need it."

Then, in spite of the protests of his wife, he got up and
hurried to the Colonel's headquarters.

*
* *

" Well, well," the Colonel said to his miserable interpreter with a sneer ; " who was right—you or I ? Who
knows the psychology of Scots better ? And who looks a
fool now ? "

" Really, I can't understand it, sir. That day the man
seemed so in agony at the very idea."

" And now, do you know, he actually pesters me ? We
flooded the pasture and a few gardens. They said it was
not enough. We cut down the alders, leaving just three,
so that the youngsters may have some place to take their
girls for a walk. We understand the needs of human
nature. But the Scots are asking us to cut down all the
trees. I left a bit of the old ruin which was not in the way.
On the contrary, it might serve as a decoy to attract German
fire. And the councillors insist on dynamiting even that
last wall. We dug a huge ditch, reinforced with timbers—
they just looked at it and said : ' Oh ! that's not deep enough ;
couldn't you make it wider ? ' If you blew up half of the
town and flooded the rest, they would feel perfectly happy.
Do you remember France ? The German tanks were
already coming and they still refused to fell trees across
the road."

" That is exactly why . . ."

" That is why it happened. But it's very different here.
They seem quiet, peaceful people, ignorant of war, nature-

loving, thrifty, cautious. Now they incurred by their own choice some expense, much inconvenience and the risk of destruction. If the Germans should ever come here, they are sure to burn down the whole town."

" Will they come ? "

" Our business is preparation, not prophecy. But do you know what is worrying them ? Not the idea that the Germans might come, but that they might not come. That they might be sunk by the Navy before they land, or smashed on the coast."

" It sounds rather odd."

" Yes, but that is precisely what is on their minds. Scotsmen don't like to spend money for nothing. They don't like to work in vain. And they have got historical sense. They realised what it would mean to win the first great victory over the Germans on the fields of Invermuchty, which we have so thoroughly prepared for the battle. A Polish-Scottish victory over the Huns, eh ? "

" A Polish victory."

" No, sir. Scots-Polish victory. They would play a tremendous part in it, I am sure. This country, although it has seen no war for centuries, has kept its fighting spirit well. It is not for nothing that they have a lion in their coat of arms and a red one, too."

* *

" You know," said the General, after listening to the whole story, " they destroyed the ruins of that abbey quite unnecessarily. I always say that a unit well provided with ' 75 ' mortars does not have to worry about dead fields. It's a failing peculiar to those who rely exclusively on machine guns—a fine weapon, no doubt, but not suited to all conditions and grounds. I wouldn't have touched those ruins. I respect ancient monuments."

" And what if the Germans did come there ? "

" Then I would give them a few well-aimed artillery salvoes."

Chapter 15

THE EARTH

" THE General told me," said the old Earl to the Major (not the member of the General's Sunday meetings), " that you are the son of a Polish Squire. I am glad that you can speak English. It will be a great pleasure to show you our old family home. Perhaps it will remind you of your own house in Poland ? "

The house, a dark castle, had little in common with the typical Polish country mansions. In Poland they used to be broad, unwilling to climb up in towers, but glad to sit well on the earth, spreading long wings on either side, in a large horseshoe-shaped quadrangle. The walls were white and there was always a porch with tall white columns.

The Earl's castle is built of grey stone, darkened with age and merging into the background of the mountains. It is Gothic rather than Classical ; there is more in it of the mediaeval cathedral than of the Hellenic colonnade ; there are still two powerful defence towers and an ancient moat. It used to be a stronghold hard to enter, unlike the Polish country house, opening its hospitable gates to all.

The rooms of the splendid Scottish home are also different. They are high—in Poland the ceilings were lower and always white, unless they were painted in gay patterns and decorated with stucco. The Scottish castle is full of dark oak panelling, which was scarce in Poland. Only the big fireplaces with logs crackling fiercely are just the same. In front of the fireplace there are heavy rugs and bearskins both in Scotland and in Poland. The sporting prints and paintings of hunting scenes on the walls are also very similar.

The old Earl, as hospitable as a Polish Squire, showed

his guests a portrait. "This was my great-great-grand-father. The upper floors were destroyed by fire in his time. That is why that part of the house is much more recent. It was rebuilt in the eighteenth century, while the part we are now in dates from the seventeenth. This portrait over the mantelpiece is of my great-grand-father, who served in the Navy. He was at Trafalgar and in Egypt."

"This is his cousin, who was our Ambassador in St. Petersburg. He brought with him a collection of bearskin rugs and the heads of the aurochs he had shot in Russia. The rugs lost most of their hair in the hundred and twenty years which have elapsed since his return, but the aurochs' heads are still in the hall.

"This is my grandfather. He took part in the quelling of the Tippo Sahib mutiny in India. He also went to Crimea and was wounded at Malakoff. It was he who brought from Greece those vases, unearthed on the Island of Chios, where Homer is supposed to have been born.

"This is our family library. There is an old book on Poland, about the marriage of a granddaughter of your King John Sobieski, who saved Vienna, to the young Stuart Pretender. My family had remained faithful to the Stuarts and one of our estates was confiscated, not to be returned until twenty years later.

"I am telling you these things, Major, because I think they might remind you of your own past. Poland is an old country; it once had its nobility and kings; it fought wars and sent ambassadors to foreign Courts. Your family, as well as mine, served its country in times of war and of peace. It also lived on the land. Probably you also have many souvenirs of your ancestors—trophies, portraits and books ? I suppose it must be very much the same thing as here ? "

*
* *

"Yes, my Lord," replied the Polish officer ; "you are right when you say that it was very much the same thing in Poland. My own family and many others have a history as old as that of English, Scottish or Irish families. We also fought in wars and served in embassies. We also loved hunting and war trophies, old books, beautiful pictures and fine armoury.

" We also had a bit of land, far from towns, but near the old family church in which we were baptised and the cemetery in which we were buried. Generations were born in the house and generations died there. But, in your country, houses of that kind remain until this day, while in my country they do not.

" I will tell you about it, if you are as interested in our country and its traditions as we are in Scotland. My family house ? It exists no longer. Russian Cossacks burnt it at the time when Thaddeus Kosciuszko fell on the battlefield and the three partitioning Powers shared our country between them, at the end of the eighteenth century.

" My great-grandfather went to Western Europe to fight there for Polish freedom. He went to Spain with Napoleon. He was at Austerlitz and Jena and on the white Moscow road. He brought back with him a captain's commission signed by the Emperor, a sword from Spain, the Legion of Honour and a wound from the Italian campaign.

" He rebuilt the house from ruins, he ploughed and he sowed. But his wound would not heal and malaria from the Ebro wore him down. He died one year before the Polish national insurrection, which broke out in 1830, when news came through that France had expelled the Bourbons, Belgium had risen against Holland, and Britain was helping Greece and other nations struggling for freedom.

" His two sons joined the insurrection. One of them was taken prisoner and sent by the Tsar to Siberia, from which he never returned. The other went abroad, a soldier exile. He fought for Italian liberty at Custozza and for Hungary at Villagos. In old age he settled in Galicia, in the South of Poland, under Austrian rule, where his wife had a smallish estate. Like his father, he built a new house, to which he brought the two family relics—the Cross of the Legion of Honour and the Spanish sword. The parchment with Napoleon's signature was lost in one of the many campaigns.

"When I was a boy, war broke out—the Great War. Our house was not far from Gorlice. The Russian artillery razed it to the ground in less than an hour. The battle went on and the Germans finished the work of destruction. After the war my father returned to where the house had been and rummaged in the rubble. The only thing he found was the Spanish sword. Rust does not bite Toledo steel.

"I did not rebuild the house. I could not afford to. My father, like my great-grandfather, tried to cure his war wounds, but never got rid of them. He only spent a good deal of money on doctors. I served in the army and lived wherever my regiment was stationed. We were first on the Latvian and Russian frontiers, then on the German one. The Spanish sword, the last family heirloom, was always with me. When this war started suddenly, I had to leave my flat in Warsaw. The house was bombed. I don't know what became of the sword.

* *
*

"You see, my Lord, how things are in Poland. There are many people like you in the United Kingdom, living on the Thames and on the Tweed, in Kent and in Wales. There are many homes like yours, though few finer, in which centuries have passed without leaving a mark other than layers of dust. But in my country all the houses are like mine, with similar family histories. Each generation lost what the previous one had saved from former disasters. Just as we lost first the accumulated wealth of hundreds of years, then the letter of commission, then the Cross, and finally even the sword.

"You had your history and we had ours. Your ancestors

once rode to battle in armour and so did ours. Your ancestors and ours were faithful to their king and collected trophies of their hunting adventures, battles and travels. But you added to your wealth and we saw ours dwindle to nothing. Your houses were consumed by fire perhaps once in three centuries. Ours were wrecked in every generation. You were sheltered by the sea. We lived among open fields. Your fortunes were different from ours.

" That is perhaps why, my Lord, we finally lost some of our love for the things for which you care and for which we once cared, too, for relics of our history. What is the good of love spent on things which every storm scatters in the wind ? It costs too much to care for what you must lose. After every conflagration, after every hurricane that has swept our land, only one thing has remained—the earth. Earth was what my great-great-grandfather found instead of home, when he returned from Spain, and what my great-grandfather found when he came to Galicia from France. And my father, when he came back after the last war, found only the soil. And I, my Lord, if I ever return, will find nothing but the bare earth. The Poles will not find their houses at home, but the bare earth alone.

" But that only makes this earth dearer to us. We have nothing else. No homes like those which wait in Scotland or Wales for the British soldier from Libya or sailor from Singapore. No treasures handed down by generations, like those to be found in every British home. No old books, or old armour or old portraits. Now perhaps you will understand that for the Pole this earth, this soil, is more than mere land. It is his home, his history, his heirloom. It is his all.

" Can you understand it, you British ? "

Chapter 16

EVERYBODY WILL BE INVITED

"I can smell spring," said Sergeant Krysta, sniffing the air in the morning ; "primroses are budding under the snow. The birds will soon come from the South."

He used to be a natural history master, and even in the army, which he joined as a volunteer, he thought in terms of seasons and natural phenomena.

"There will be more mud, damn it !" swore his neighbour in the same hut, Private (1st Class) Kowalski, an ex-Poznan taxi-driver, who escaped from Germany to join the army.

"It's going to be the second spring out of Poland," reflected, sadly, 17-year-old Private Rohoyski, who had left Poland as a schoolboy. His father, a well-known professor of medicine at Wilno University, and the owner of a small country estate, was deported by the Russians to the steppes of Kazakstan and employed there as a camel driver in the Kolchoz of the October Revolution.

"Yes, that's right," they all replied ; "perhaps it may bring us nearer to Poland ?"

It was the first warmish day on the coast and there was spring in the air. It was pleasant to go on such a day to the frozen pillboxes on the beach, to look out for Goering and Grand Admiral Raeder, a couple of old foxes, always ready to raid the poultry yard. Everyone felt strangely thrilled and romantically inclined.

"Oh ! this must be spring," observed the Major by the evening. "I feel my rheumatism again and that's a sure sign." He sat down to his whisky more thoughtfully than usual.

The whole platoon was assembled in the corrugated-steel shed, but the men were rather silent. Nobody wanted to play cards and even the radio was switched off—a slight seldom suffered by Lady Warrender's talking gifts.

A new camp sheet was just out, but no one cared to read it. There was a fresh copy of the Polish newspaper from London, with no more than five official speeches, but even that failed to excite curiosity. Somebody brought an issue of a Polish literary periodical in which not one of the authors jibed at another—but it left everybody quite cool. Another man had an English Sunday paper with an article by H. G. Wells, in which he neither attacked the Pope and the Poles, nor glorified Kremlin democracy. But the public in the hut remained adamant and unthrilled.

"What are you thinking about?" Sergeant Krysta asked young Rohoyski ; he was feeling somewhat paternal towards the youngest lad in the platoon and sometimes thought he was one of the boys in his class.

"Me?" said Rohoyski, surprised. "Me? Nothing, just some silly nonsense. . . . Somebody said to-day that this spring brings us nearer to Poland. So I was wondering what it will be like in Poland and what I will do first. . . ."

"Good idea," said the schoolmaster. "Well, let's all think about what we would do first after returning home and what we shall do when we get back. I give you five minutes to make plans and then you must tell them!"

There was again silence in the big hut, lit by a few flickering oil lamps.

*
* *

"The five minutes are up," announced the ex-natural history master of Gdynia. "Now you will all speak in turn."

"I will buy a new taxi," said Kowalski ; "a British one, like those I saw in Edinburgh. They are well made. You must have seen them, too."

"I," said Bochnak, "will finish my work on the influence of Horace on Polish Renaissance poets. I hope my mother saved the manuscript, because the house in Warsaw was not destroyed."

Like many Polish soldiers he was a scholar.

" I," said Rohoyski, " will rebuild our house in the country, which the Bolsheviks knocked own, pretending that they needed the bricks for a school, which they never put up after all."

" Me," said Burkat. " I will get drunk."

" Everyone will do what he can do best," observed the impartial schoolmaster ; " but Burkat's answer seems incomplete. Of course, we shall all get drunk on that day. . . ."

" Ah ! " said Burkat, in defence of his plan, " but I will do better than ordinary. I heard that vodka is cheap under the Germans. But I can't believe so much good of them."

" I think it is true," said Krysta, " for the Germans want to drug the nation with alcohol, while the Polish Governments kept the price of spirits up to prevent drunkenness. . . ."

" It's a good idea " (Burkat cheered up) ; " and I suppose they won't have time to put up the price again at once."

The plans for the future would probably have stuck there if it had not been for Karp, who said, calmly, from his bed :

" I will ask the Smiths from Castle Street to Poland."

The idea struck like a thunderbolt, opening up a field of new possibilities.

" Whom will you ask ? " inquired Rohoyski, unbelievingly.

" The Smiths. You know them as well as I do. Castle Street. Where we had tea last week. I will ask them."

" What ? Not all the Smiths ? Surely not Grandma ? "

" All of them ! Grandma Smith, too."

" You're crazy ! She can hardly walk."

" It does not matter. She will go by boat and then we'll carry her."

" But they never would go as far as that."

This remark enraged Burkat. " What do you mean ?
Won't they ? I could come to Scotland, and they can
come to Poland just as well. Wouldn't they go to
Limanowa ? You will see that when I ask them they will
come."

" In any case," said Kowalski, with quiet dignity, " they
will have to come to me, too. And I was their guest
before you were, so they really should come to me first."

Burkat was furious. " First ? Who thought of asking
them ? Not you. You were just thinking about your ——
taxi in Poznan. . . ."

" Quiet, please," said Krysta, exactly as though he was
taking his class in natural history. " You need not quarrel
about who is going to ask the full Smith family first.
I will tell you something—*we shall ask everybody*."

And he looked round, rather pleased with himself, as if
he had just explained to the boys some particularly interesting natural phenomenon.

" What do you mean—everybody ? " asked Burkat,
indignantly, who was looking forward to a monopoly of
asking Scots to Poland.

" Everybody," said the schoolmaster, beaming. " We
shall ask all the Scots to return our visit. When Poland
is free again and we have returned, we shall say to the
Scots : ' We were in many countries and we ate the bread
of many nations through the long years of war and exile.
Some bread was tough and some was salty, some was bitter
and some stuck in our throats, for the bread of an exile in
foreign lands does not often taste sweet. . . .' "

" Stop preaching ! " grunted Kowalski, who felt a kind
of lump in his throat.

" Let him ! " said Galica. It was too dark to see his eyes.

" Then we'll say to the Scots," carried on the schoolmaster, Sergeant Krysta : ' Your bread was the best, for
it was given willingly and with a kind heart, not like a
pittance. . . .' "

" . . . Don't talk like that, old chap," said Kowalski.

" ' . . . but like a loaf shared with a brother and friend. You did not even know us and yet you treated us like brothers.' "

" Honest truth," endorsed Burkat.

" 'So now come to us, so that you may know us at last. After victory we want you all to come to Poland.' "

" But how can you ask them all ? Not all the Scotsmen ? "

But the ex-schoolmaster went on, as though he had an important lecture to make.

" All the Scots. Everyone that wants to come. Even strangers, even those who paid so gladly for the drinks of unknown Polish soldiers when they met them in bars. . . .

" We'll show them some drinks ! " said Burkat, with a misty look of delight in his eye.

" And the Scottish ladies, the old women and the girls who asked us, strangers, in for tea with good cakes and a warm fire and a warm, friendly smile. . . ."

" They must come," said Kowalski.

" And the little children, who asked for souvenirs, who learned to say in Polish : good-day, good-night, good-bye, cheerio everybody."

" And Professor Sarolea, who has been for over twenty years our greatest friend in Scotland . . ."

" Yes, yes." The whole platoon nodded approval.

" And Lady Warrender, who gave us, even when we were in France, no end of Gillettes, socks, wireless sets, cigarettes . . ."

" Yes, yes, yes ! "

" And all the girls from the Y.M.C.A. canteen, who were so nice to talk to . . ."

" Yes, yes ! "

" And the young ladies of St. Andrews who organised a canteen for us."

" And those of Dundee . . ."

" And of Glasgow . . ."

" And Forfar . . ."

" And from Perth ! "

" And finally, my friends, we shall ask our best friend in this country, that model host, Sir Patrick Dollan, Lord Provost of Glasgow," said Sergeant Krysta with solemnity.

A roar went up, as after the scoring of a much-desired goal, a popular knockout or the favourite's victory on the racecourse. The steel hut rang with loud cheers and everybody started shouting at the top of their voices : " Yes, we want Dollan."

" Give us our Dollan," yelled Kowalski.

" Good old Dollanowski," cried Burkat, using the approved Polish version of the name.

Then everybody shouted the names of their prospective guests, anxious to be in before the others.

" And the Macmillans ! "

" And Macdonald from Kirriemuir ! "

" And Forsyte ! "

" And those two girls from the farm ! "

" And our postmaster ! "

" And the girl from the pub ! "

" Her father, too ! "

" And those British soldiers from Bridge of Earn whom we had a scrap with about that red-haired minx ! "

" And the King and Queen ! "

" Churchill ! "

" Gentlemen," said Sergeant Krysta at this point, again in the part of the schoolmaster keeping wild boys in hand ; " I don't think you should speak about the King and Queen and a man like the present Prime Minister in such a way. I see what you mean and I feel the same way myself, but you can be sure that they will be asked to Wawel Castle and entertained in our royal house by the President. Don't worry about asking them ! What we want is a real friendship between two nations and between people. That will be the result of our visit to Scotland and their return visit to Poland."

" Hurrah, hurrah, hurray ! "

The Adjutant and three officers rushed into the hut.

" What is the meaning of this row ?   Drinking, eh ?
You will report to the Colonel ! "

There was dead silence.

" You've chosen your time well.   The General has just
arrived for a surprise inspection.   Well . . ."

" What was it ? " asked the General, appearing in the
doorway.   " Who is the senior here ?   Sergeant Krysta ?
And you, Sergeant, allow things like this ?   You a
schoolmaster ? "

" When I came in he was up and shouting like mad,"
reported the Adjutant, officiously.

" What has come over you ? " asked the General, who
realised that this was no common occurrence.   " What,
you weren't even drinking !   That's very suspicious," he
said, seeing no bottles about.

Assisted by the others, poor Sergeant Krysta mumbled
out the reasons for the noisy celebration.

The General listened and then said: " It's all very well,
but you should not make noise at night.   You will report
to-morrow to your Battalion Commander."

* *

But, walking back to his car, he said to the Colonel :
" When they report to you to-morrow, don't do them any
harm.   I had to scare them a bit, but it really does not
matter."

" Perhaps three days' strict ? " suggested the Colonel,
eagerly.

" No, I should let them off," replied the General.

In the car he said to his Aide-de-Camp : " Our learned
Cadet does not seem to be doing anything at all, you
know."

" Well, sir, he translates British regulations ; he carries
on the whole English correspondence and now he . . ."

" What is it ? " interrupted the General.   " When I was
his age I could do three times as much !   No, we must get

him going. He must write for our camp sheet a—what do
you call it ?—a vision. Yes, a vision. Something about
what the mass visit of Scots to Poland will look like."

" I will tell him, sir."

Chapter 17

THE GREAT DAY

" FROM early morning "—the Cadet was reading his " vision "—" all the cliffs, all the quays and jetties, even all the roofs of the city and the white hill of Oksywie, which had resisted the enemy for many weeks; in fact the whole of Gdynia . . ."

" Excuse me," broke in the Major, " it should not be Gdynia. We will meet them in Szczecin (Stettin) or Krolewiec (Königsberg), ports built by the Germans on land robbed from us and surrounded by villages in which there are still Slav peasants. . . ."

" There will be a fine for interruptions as usual," said the General. " I think that Gdynia, a place which was a small village under the Germans and was turned by the Poles into the largest port in the Baltic, is really quite suitable."

" . . . the whole of Gdynia was filled with cheerful crowds. Special trains from all over Poland brought thousands of men, women and children. Many of them stayed in nearby Danzig. There were so many that some had to sleep in railway carriages and tents. But they waited."

" I am sure it will be like that," observed the Colonel.

" Shortly before ten o'clock small black dots appeared on the horizon. The sea was smooth and nearly blue. At that moment all the sirens in the harbour and all the church bells began to welcome the visitors. Those of Danzig, Warsaw, Poznan, Cracow, Lwow and Wilno did, too, although they could not be heard.

" And the bells of every village. . . ." said the Padre.

" Yes, of every village," continued the Cadet. " And

the guns of Oksywie, which drove back in September, 1939, many German attacks, and those of Westerplatte, a proud Alcazar, and those of Hel fired a royal salute."

" It will be a pleasant reminder of the good old war days," said the General.

" Fine liners, escorted by Polish warships, were approaching the port. Their decks were lined with Scots scanning eagerly the Polish coast and looking with interest at the escorting cruisers, ' George VI,' ' Churchill ' and ' Scotland,' built in Britain during the last year of the war, for the Polish Navy, and named in memory of the days of common danger and struggle."

" I must make a note of that," observed the General.

" The children were quick to point out landmarks on the coast, which they knew well from books and from the stories of Polish soldiers which they had heard in Scotland. They pointed to a long, thin peninsula covered with pine forest : ' Look, mummy ! this is Hel. That's where they fought the Germans until they had no more ammunition and only a few men left. You know, I told you about it.' "

" ' Oh, yes,' replied the mother, who did not remember the story at all ; ' it's a lovely forest.'

" ' Look, that's Danzig over there on the left ! '

" ' Why can't we see Westerplatte ? '

" ' Hurray ! this is Gdynia ! '

" The young Scots knew everything. When one liner after another entered the port they yelled until they were hoarse : ' Czolem ! Czolem ! Dzien dobry ! Dzien dobry ! '

" On the other side, on land, there were just as many Polish children, who cried in English : ' Long live Scotland ! '

" But soon it was the loudspeakers which began to make the noise. Everyone in Poland and in Scotland was listening to the transmission from Gdynia. But amidst the general enthusiasm and cheering nobody heard the very long and elaborate speeches which the Polish notables had prepared for the occasion. People just saw their lips moving."

" That was wonderful," said the Major.

" Everyone was busy looking for his own friends. A certain Major, by that time promoted to Colonel, was seen embracing an Alistair McDonald, hotel owner from St. Andrews. . . ."

" That's about me." The Major spotted himself with his usual brightness. " It's old McDonald with whom we always have two double gins."

" And a jolly military Chaplain was seen to kiss on both cheeks a pale-eyed Minister of a parish not far from Dundee. . . ."

" That's me, by God ! " gasped the Padre.

" Everybody was discovering his most congenial companion in the other nation. The more prominent of the guests were specially welcomed on land. At that moment the radio commentator at last had his chance :

" ' And now we see,' he said, ' a tall, handsome man in a red ermine-lined gown. He is just setting foot on shore. This man is . . .'

" Dollan ! Dollan ! " the crowd was cheering with a roar.

" ' This man,' continued the radio commentator for the benefit of the listeners who could not see the great moment, ' is no other than . . .'

" ' Why does he have to say it ? ' fumed millions of Poles at their loudspeakers ; ' don't we know well enough that it's the Lord Provost of Glasgow, Sir Patrick Dollan ? '

" ' And here,' yelled the tireless announcer, ' comes a tall lady, very straight in her A.T.S. uniform, with a charming smile. . . .'

" ' Idiot ! ' muttered the listeners, ' does he really think we don't know what Lady Warrender looks like ? '

" ' And now . . .' went on the patient radio voice, describing all the eminent visitors and trying to speak above the cheerful noise of the crowd.

Everybody was talking at once, at the top of their voices. After all, they were in Poland.

' You remember that girl at the pictures in Perth ? ' said a Scot to a Pole.

' Yes, of course, I remember her.'

' Well, she got married.'

' Did she ? And who is the lucky fellow ? '

But other friends broke in.

' Don't you remember me? You're old Bill of Earn !'

' Not as old as all that ! '

' Of course not. We trained on your farm. Is it still as muddy as it used to be ? '

' It is, but now I've got a field of potatoes there.'

' And how are things in Forfar ? '

' And in Blairgowrie ? '

' And in Perth ? '

' And what about Cupar ? '

' How is your Jar . . . Jarocin ? '

' Do you still live in Newport ? '

' Does Elsie still work in the café ? '

Some of the Scots put up a counter-barrage of questions.

' So you've got married ? '

' How is business in Warsaw ? '

' Do you like civilian life ? '

' How is your old wound in the leg ? '

' And you did find your family after all ! Wasn't I right when I told you they were safe ? '

" ' But why do we stand here talking in the open when there are plenty of places to go to ? ' said one of the more sensible Poles. ' Let's try some *czysta wyborowa* or bitter vodka.'

" There was no shortage of refreshments. Large quantities of Scotch were provided for the occasion, to make the guests feel at home. Besides, the Poles returning from Scotland had brought with them an extended knowledge of drinks, adding to the already wide assortment of Polish cellars."

" Nothing brings the nations closer together than drink,"
observed the Major, sententiously.

" And war," added the General.

" The younger generation of the two countries was
also getting along together very well, without the assistance
of Scotch and Czysta.

" ' Daddy ! ' cried a six-year-old, ' show me Jack you
told me so much about. You know, you gave him a white
eagle and he reminded you of me ? '

" ' But how can I find him ? ' replied the harassed
father, ' with hundreds of kids all alike ? '

" ' But I want to see Jack ! '

" Most of the Polish children were not so particular.
They were glad to meet any of the young Scots. ' Do you
like Poland ? ' they asked, eagerly.

" ' Yes, yes ! ' replied the young Scots, before having
seen anything. ' Where is the Wawel ? Is this really
Gdynia ? I know about Gdynia. I know how the Germans
tried to drive you all out of it in the winter, through the
snow.'

" ' How did you know about it ? ' wondered the Polish
children. ' The Germans did not want you to know those
things. But now it's all over. You will stay with us.'

*
* *

" After the first few days," the Cadet continued, reading
his account of the future, " when the welcome was over,
the Poles told the Scots : ' Ladies, gentlemen and children,
you will now go inland. Each of you will be the guest of
a Polish family, either of people you already know, or of
their friends, or just of Poles who have heard that in their
long wanderings in evil times the Polish soldiers never
found more friendly hospitality than in Scotland. They
want to return this hospitality, and that is why we asked all
who could come. Stay as long as you like. You will get
to know us. You may not always be very comfortable, for
the country is still making good the terrible destruction
of the war and of years of hostile exploitation. You will

see us at work. You may be able to help us with a word
of advice. There may be opportunities for business
collaboration. But that is by the way. Even if you see
us poor, you will know that we are happy, for we are
rebuilding our homes on our own land. May this be the
last time we have to rebuild them.' Amen."

" I don't like that ending very much," said the Colonel ;
" it does not sound practical. I would have said : ' On
Tuesday next Scotland will play Poland at football in
Warsaw. On Wednesday the open golf championship of
Poland will begin at Cracow, with the best Scottish players
taking part. On Thursday there will be played in Poznan
a lawn tennis match between the national teams. There
will also be angling competitions on the Poprad, the
Wislok and the Sola, which are full of ten-pound trout.'
That sort of thing would make the Scots feel that they were
coming to a civilised country."

" I am afraid," said the glum Padre, " that there will be
among the visitors many girls to whom our men promised
marriage, and not a few creditors . . ."

" Everything will be provided," said the General.
" There will be sport of every kind. We shall have trout
and salmon even in the Vistula. As to shooting, it has
always been excellent. And the Scottish lassies will be so
popular in Poland after the war that there will be ten boys
to choose from for every disappointed girl landing in
Gdynia."